The Virtual Sales Handbook

The Virtual Sales Handbook

A Hands-on Approach to Engaging Customers

Mante Kvedare
Christian Milner Nymand

WILEY

This work was produced in collaboration with Write Business Results Limited. For more information on Write Business Results' business book, blog, and podcast services, please visit their website: www.writebusinessresults.com, email us on info@ writebusinessresults.com or call us on 020 3752 7057.

Registered office
John Wiley & Sons Ltd, The Atrium, Southern Gate, Chichester, West Sussex, PO19 8SQ, United Kingdom

For details of our global editorial offices, for customer services and for information about how to apply for permission to reuse the copyright material in this book please see our website at www.wiley.com.

Library of Congress Cataloging-in-Publication Data

Names: Kvedare, Mante, author. | Nymand, Christian Milner, author.
Title: The virtual sales handbook : a hands-on approach to engaging
    customers / Mante Kvedare, Christian Milner Nymand.
Description: [Hoboken, NJ] : Wiley, 2021. | Includes index.
Identifiers: LCCN 2020046370 (print) | LCCN 2020046371 (ebook) | ISBN
    9781119775768 (hardback) | ISBN 9781119775904 (adobe pdf) | ISBN
    9781119775898 (epub)
Subjects: LCSH: Electronic commerce. | Selling. | Internet marketing. |
    Customer relations.
Classification: LCC HF5548.32 .K88 2021 (print) | LCC HF5548.32 (ebook) |
    DDC 658.8/72—dc23
LC record available at https://lccn.loc.gov/2020046370
LC ebook record available at https://lccn.loc.gov/2020046371

Cover Design: Wiley
Cover Illustration: Implement Consulting Group,
Background Image © Eakachai Leesin/EyeEm/Getty Images

Set in 12/16pt Janson Text LT Std by SPi Global, Chennai, India
Printed and bound by CPI Group (UK) Ltd, Croydon, CR0 4YY

10 9 8 7 6 5 4 3 2 1

To the reader, who wants to start navigating the virtual sales world.

Contents

Preface

The Virtual Sales Handbook is a hands-on guide for sales profes-sionals introducing the basics of effective virtual customer engagement. It explores the opportunity space of embracing the virtual medium, as well as the barriers associated with virtual meetings and how to effectively overcome them.

This book provides hands-on tips and tricks on how to effectively prepare, run, and follow up on virtual meetings, and inspiration on leading the transformation from physical to vir-tual sales in a hybrid sales model.

During the past 15 years, we have had the privilege of work-ing with commercial organisations all over the world and met thousands of dedicated sales people, who, on a daily basis, aim to help and inspire their customers and inspire their current and prospective customers.

We want to dedicate this book to all of you, and we hope the recommendations, tips, and tricks introduced can help you all increase your reach and impact.

We also hope that by applying more virtual interactions, you are all able to create better results whilst freeing up more time to spend with your friends and relatives. We hope you will see Virtual Customer Engagement as a true win-win concept, benefitting both your customers, yourself, the planet, and your friends and family.

Introduction

I cannot wait to get back to physical meetings again.

How often have you thought that in recent months? If you have, then you are certainly not alone! One question we often hear is: "Are virtual sales meetings as good as sales meetings conducted in person?"

There are certain things that cannot be fully replaced by technology. Most salespeople prefer face-to-face contact with customers and prospects for many good reasons. Behavioural science argues that the best way to gain someone's trust is by being together physically. The reason is that trust between people is built as a result of nonverbal cues like facial expressions, body language, the positioning of someone's hands, and so on.

There is a reason why sales is often regarded as an art as much as a science —and many salespeople rely on their interpersonal relationships and their personal charisma as much as they rely on their hard sales skills. Interacting with physical distance, for example, via a phone or virtual interface like Zoom, Teams, Skype or others, limits most of these nonverbal cues and can make it more difficult to leverage our "soft skills."

However, the recent global pandemic has forced us to acknowledge that we need to find a way to adapt to a primarily virtual environment for customer and prospect interactions. With social distancing likely to be something we must accept for months or even years to come, we need to ask a fundamentally different question: **How can you make virtual sales meetings as good as face-to-face sales meetings?**

That is what this handbook is designed to help you achieve—making your virtual customer and sales meetings as good as, or even better than, face-to-face meetings. Over the coming chapters, we share advice, tips, and tricks to allow you to master virtual selling and virtual customer interactions to the same extent that you master face-to-face interactions. If you follow our recommendations, we are sure you will conclude that virtual sales and customer meetings can be as successful as face-to-face meetings. What is more, we are also confident that you will realise you can produce the same or better results all while freeing up more time for your family, friends, and hobbies.

Virtual selling is a win-win concept. You will benefit, your customers will benefit, and even the planet will benefit.

But I already had virtual meetings before Covid-19—what is new?

If you follow some of the global research on the adoption of virtual selling, you will already know that more than 50% of salespeople already held virtual meetings before the pandemic.[1] So, what has changed? What is new?

We believe there are three major paradigm shifts taking place:

1. **Virtual is often the only option:** Before Covid-19, it was you who decided which meetings were fit for virtual and which were not. During the period of social distancing and/or lockdown, most of us were forced to conduct all our meetings virtually. This included the ones that we would usually have held as face-to-face meetings. Now we no longer have the power to make that decision.
   Some meetings will be with people in countries you cannot travel to either due to local travel bans or because of the

risk that you have to self-quarantine on your return home. And even when national or regional border restrictions are lifted, many sales organisations believe that their customers will remain reluctant to welcome external partners on site in the long run—making effective virtual customer engagement a precondition to effectively serve your customer base. In our recent study of over 300 global commercial employees, 80% admitted that they would continue to use virtual as a means to connect with customers and prospects in the future.

of commercial employees admitted they would continue to use virtual sales in the future

2. **Technology and technology adoption are picking up:** Think back to the early days of the pandemic. Most people did not turn on their camera in virtual meetings, and you were probably amazed when someone seamlessly navigated between PowerPoint, chat, and breakout rooms (in Zoom). Two things have happened since early March 2020. Most people have gotten used to the technology and can now use several basic functions to make virtual meetings work better, including turning on the camera and uploading a PowerPoint presentation. At the same time, the virtual platforms have improved. There is no doubt that Microsoft Teams was behind Zoom in March 2020, but with the recent releases, technology is certainly becoming more supportive in making virtual interactions work even better.

The adoption of new technology and new ways of working follow a predictable path. First, you see innovators trying new technologies and ways of working simply because they are new and different. The early adopters follow the innovators and are then followed by the early majority. The late majority join next and finally the laggards come on board. In our recent virtual sales study, we found that 80% of respondents can be classified as virtual embracers or late adopters: commercial employees characterised by their willingness to pursue more virtual customer meetings in the future. Only 20% were classified as virtual resistors—those who expect to go fully back to a physical "normal" face-to-face model once the pandemic has ceased.

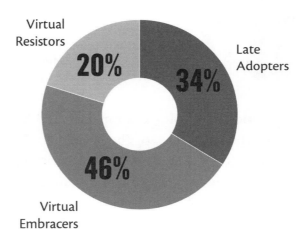

● 46% Virtual Embracers
Respondents who will pursue the virtual engagement model in the future.

● 34% Late Adopters
Respondents who will pursue the virtual engagement model in the future.

● 20% Virtual Resistors
Respondents who will not pursue the virtual engagement model in the future.

3. **More people better adjust their approach to fit virtual delivery:** Pre-Covid-19, studies showed that more than 50% of salespeople believed they adjusted their behaviour and how they interacted online to fit virtual interaction. However, when observed, experts revealed that just 12% adjusted properly[2] and used the necessary tools to make the most of a virtual interaction. That means, unless you were among the 12%, there was plenty of opportunity to improve the quality and outcome of virtual meetings.

Following eight intense months (March 2020 to October 2020) of applying virtual tools, being in virtual meetings both internally and externally, and attending various virtual training and knowledge-sharing sessions, we believe this number has changed. We see a higher proportion of salespeople adapting more of the tools and practices driving effective customer meetings. As a result, quite a large proportion of respondents in our survey now find that virtual meetings are as effective or even slightly better than the face-to-face meetings they held previously. Of close to 300 respondents, 48% replied that virtual meetings are as good or better than previous meetings and that they are likely to continue working virtually and increasing their number of meetings altogether going forward.

Are you saying that the future of sales is fully virtual?

No! Absolutely not. We recently interviewed Mark Bowden, an expert in human psychology and body language, and asked him the question: Can we expect a future of 100% virtual sales meetings?

This was his answer: *"In any sales situation, the person who gets in front of the customer will win the deal."*

He shared plenty of examples of why it is still so important to have that face-to-face contact, many of which related to the importance of non-verbal communication and creating trust between people. We also do not believe in a fully virtual sales model for most companies. The human factor is simply too important to be fully replaced with a screen. What we do believe, however, is in the future of a hybrid model. The hybrid model leverages each mode of customer interaction—both physical and virtual—for its strengths: to secure the most impactful, effective, and engaging customer experience possible. It is a future where we innovate our virtual and physical meetings to deliver high value to our customers and prospects.

The opportunities are endless. As we move through the book, we will touch on these potential ways of using the virtual world to innovate and create new ways of meeting and creating value for customers and prospects.

How comfortable are you in virtual sales meetings?

Our research found that virtual meeting success is strongly correlated with salespeople's virtual comfort level: those with the highest comfort levels (8.0/10) report better virtual meeting outcomes than even face-to-face, while those with the lowest average comfort level (6.3/10) report experiencing worse outcomes when interacting virtually.

We will explore this idea of comfort later in the book, but the reason we are telling you this is because how you rate your comfort level appears to be key to the level of success you have in virtual meetings. If you are not comfortable with hosting meetings in a virtual environment, then it is not realistic to expect them to go well.

The good news is that your comfort level can be improved through training and rehearsals. So, if you find yourself in the category of seeing worse outcomes from virtual meetings, you may take comfort in the fact that further training and more frequent "just trying it out" will eventually lead you to also see the full benefits, just as 80% (early adopters and late adopters) of your colleagues already do, according to our research.

One of our main motivations in writing this book is to help you improve your comfort level in the virtual environment. If we can get everyone who reads this book to a comfort level of eight or above, we will feel that we have done a good job.

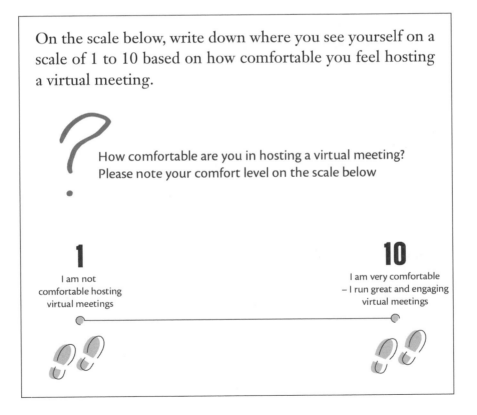

On the scale below, write down where you see yourself on a scale of 1 to 10 based on how comfortable you feel hosting a virtual meeting.

How comfortable are you in hosting a virtual meeting? Please note your comfort level on the scale below

1

I am not
comfortable hosting
virtual meetings

10

I am very comfortable
– I run great and engaging
virtual meetings

Tap into our expertise

As well as extensive experience in sales, we have a great deal of knowledge to share about introducing and facilitating virtual sales meetings.

Christian Milner Nymand and Mante Kvedare are both Partners at Implement Consulting Group, where they have been driving the business' virtual sales initiatives, contributing to thought leadership on the topic of virtual selling, and leading training programs for global commercial managers.

Christian joined Implement in 2003 after working as a management consultant at a Danish consulting company. In his role as senior partner, he helps global B2B companies improve their commercial capabilities and accelerate their top-line growth. He is highly competent at operationalising commercial, sales, and marketing excellence methods and tools to create business impact. He has led several global sales transformation projects as a result of his extensive knowledge and experience.

Mante has more than 10 years of experience in supporting international organisations in commercial transformations. Prior to joining Implement, she managed a business unit for a key Nordic FMCG player. Her primary focus is on developing the commercial agenda of B2C and B2B companies, where she successfully delivers change initiatives as a trusted advisor to the C-suite. Her experience of working with organisations across Europe, the Middle East, and Asia gives her a strong cross-cultural understanding and a global viewpoint.

Our aim with this book is to help you feel more comfortable operating in a virtual sales environment, as well as to introduce you to the various opportunities that virtual selling offers. We will explore the key barriers to good virtual meetings, providing you with actionable tips and tricks to help you overcome some of the most common issues we have identified.

We have designed this book to be highly practical, providing you with useful tools and tips that you can introduce to your meetings immediately. As we move through the chapters, we will explore how to prepare for and deliver a successful virtual sales meeting, with a particular focus on building engagement and trust with your customers.

We will also dive into the hybrid sales model, looking at what this means for the future of sales and how you and your organisation can combine the best of the virtual and physical worlds to deliver added value to your customers.

Chapter 1:

NAVIGATING THE WORLD OF VIRTUAL SALES

Adjusting to a new reality

As Kim reached for her alarm that was buzzing at 6:30 am, she had a strange feeling in her stomach. It wasn't the usual urge for a cup of strong coffee, it was a feeling as though she had woken up in a new reality.

Memories came flooding back, like news flashes. The night before the Prime Minister had announced a total lockdown across the country. She could picture fragments of the headlines: "Stay at home," "Global pandemic," "Save lives." Everyone had to stay at home if possible, and all the schools in the country were closed for a minimum of four weeks. They'd all seen it coming, the gradual creep of Covid-19 cases that was turning into a flood. Still, the realisation that nothing was normal hit her like a ton of bricks, while she was lying still wrapped in her duvet.

She shook her head, as if trying to shake the headlines out of her brain, and turned to her phone. This was how she always started her day. A quick scan of her calendar to get an overview of what lay ahead for the day. She was suddenly relieved that this week her ex-husband had their kids. *At least I'll have time to work, even if it is from home.* Kim was still looking at her phone as she rolled toward the side of the bed. She tapped into one entry in her diary at 10 am, and she half smiled. *My most important meeting of the year so far. When I close this deal, I'll be over my target … and I'll get a nice bonus.*

Kim's thoughts were interrupted abruptly and painfully as she tripped, slamming her head into the wall. Her phone clattered to the floor. She'd been so preoccupied thinking about the meeting, her desire for a strong coffee, and her uncertainty about this new normal that she'd forgotten about the step around the bed. *Who the hell puts a bed on a platform?!* She winced as she gingerly brought her fingers up to her forehead. At least there was no blood.

In her kitchen, Kim brewed her coffee and retrieved an ice pack from the freezer, placing it carefully against her now throbbing forehead. Sitting on a stool at her kitchen island, one hand holding the ice pack, she decided to take control of the situation. It was only 7:30 am. She tapped out a quick message to her contact for her 10 am meeting.

"Hi Paul, I hope you had a good night's sleep, despite the Prime Minister's announcement yesterday. I assume we are not safe to meet in person given the Covid-19 situation? Or what do you think? I am open to any suggestion you may have about how we can make this meeting today work despite the lockdown. Kind regards, Kim."

One of the things she loved about her new phone was that it displayed when someone was in the process of replying to a text message. She saw the reassuring blue text "typing" appear in the corner of the screen just moments after hitting send. She could hear her heart in her ears. She put her phone on the counter and reached for her mug of coffee, taking a long, slow sip to steady her nerves. *I don't know what he'll suggest. I hope we can still go ahead with this meeting. It would make my year! And it would make the bump on the head hurt a little less …. Maybe I could use some of my bonus to get rid of that stupid raised bed?* Kim realised the ice pack wasn't doing enough, and that she'd need to go in search of painkillers soon.

"Beep!" The sound almost made Kim jump, even though she'd been expecting it. She took a deep breath before opening Paul's reply. It was a short message, despite how long it had taken him to respond.

"Hi Kim,

We will make it a virtual meeting instead. I will email you a link to a Zoom meeting half an hour before the meeting. Paul"

Kim's heart sank. *Uh-oh, a virtual meeting* …. Kim was one of the most successful salespeople in her team, and she was widely admired for her ability to connect with customers, manage even the most complicated negotiations, and close the biggest deals. Face-to-face meetings had always been Kim's strong point, and, until now, she'd successfully been able to avoid virtual meetings, where she felt that it would be difficult to leverage her strong in-person impact virtually. *How am I going to shine in a virtual meeting, through a screen?*

She finished her coffee, stood and made her way to the bathroom in search of painkillers for her now pounding headache. As she looked at herself in the mirror, she realised that a virtual meeting could be a blessing in disguise; a large bulge had become quite visible on her forehead and was turning a vivid blue and purple colour. *Maybe today of all days this virtual meeting is a blessing. I can't wait to get back to physical meetings once this is all over, though!*

Kim turned away from examining her forehead and started to run a bath. She left the taps running to go and make herself a second cup of coffee. Although the bath helped her feel a little more relaxed, it did little to get rid of the slightly sick feeling in her stomach and her, now slightly dulled, headache. Examining the bump in the mirror again, she did her best to cover it with makeup, but wasn't overly worried that it was still pretty prominent as it was going to be a virtual meeting anyway.

She turned on her PC to log into her emails and see if Paul had shared the Zoom link for the meeting. It was ready, waiting at the top of her inbox. She clicked into it and instantly cursed as she read Paul's email. *Why didn't I pay more attention when I was getting out of bed this morning?!*

Dear Kim,
As agreed, find below a link to our upcoming virtual meeting.
Please turn your camera on during the meeting.
Regards,
Paul

A world of change

Virtual selling is becoming more commonplace, with a growing number of businesses realising that they need to adapt and learn how to sell in the virtual as well as the physical world. Our research found that 70% of companies are likely to run virtual customer meetings in the future.

The Covid-19 crisis has significantly accelerated this process. It has fundamentally changed the way in which B2B (business to business) companies interact with their customers. Overnight, businesses had to transition from face-to-face meetings to virtual customer interactions.

The sales industry has changed forever. This is not simply something that will go back to "normal" once travel restrictions are lifted. In fact, corporate travel is expected to remain extremely limited until 2023,[1] and quite possibly beyond. Even when national or regional border restrictions are lifted, many commercial organisations expect that their customers will be reluctant to welcome external partners on their premises.

While the rash transition to a primarily virtual customer engagement model has been a shock to many organisations and salespeople, it has presented a significant opportunity for those who are prepared to embrace virtual selling to transform their business model for a more sustainable, efficient, and cost-effective future.

Do the benefits of virtual selling outweigh the hassle?

Virtual selling presents many opportunities for businesses that do it well. It has benefits in four main areas: for you, for your customers, for your company, and for the planet.

Benefits of virtual sales

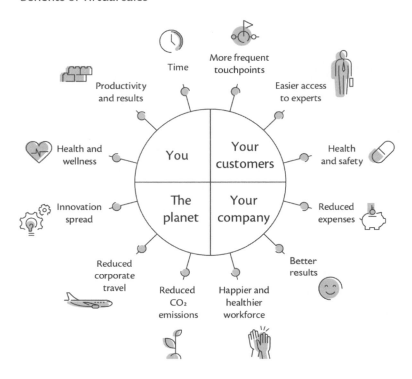

Benefits for you

There are three main areas where adopting virtual selling will benefit you as a salesperson: time, productivity and results, and health and wellness.

Time

Did you know that over half of business travellers state that being away from home for work impacts their personal lives?[2] Or that less than 30% of business travellers believe that it is optimal to travel for work more than once a quarter?[3]

Virtual selling frees up your time, and you can use that additional time in two ways. The first is to do more work without having to work more hours. The time that you used to spend travelling could now be spent holding additional meetings.

The second is to use this additional time to spend more time with your family and friends, or doing hobbies that you enjoy. Both options will help give you a better balance between your work and personal lives. In our recent study of more than 300 global commercial managers, respondents self-reported that transitioning toward more virtual interactions allowed them to save up to 20% of their working time.

of working time can be saved by transitioning toward more virtual interactions

Productivity and results

When you adopt a virtual selling model you can increase the number of meetings you have with your clients while using fewer resources. In a traditional sales model, you and your team will spend 40% of your time travelling, 30% of your time with customers, and 30% of your time on admin and associated tasks.[4]

When you switch to a virtual sales model, you can reduce the amount of time you and your team spend travelling by half. This can be poured into more time with your customers. All of a sudden, 50% of your time is with customers, 20% is travelling, and 30% is admin and associated tasks. We estimate that this can result in a 35% increase in revenue.

Virtual selling also allows you to increase your reach. In the past, you might have avoided booking meetings with clients who are in remote locations that are difficult to travel to. It was simply too difficult to find the time to make the trip, and the potential upside did not outweigh the hassle. By turning remote physical meetings into virtual interactions, you can increase your customer reach and potentially expand your customer portfolio—without the time and expense of corporate travel.

It also allows you to extend your reach to other countries and into places in other time zones. It is not only that it is easier to connect with your existing clients who are in remote locations; it is also easier to reach out to potential new clients in other locations. Virtual selling opens up a world of clients—eliminating geographical boundaries. Although you have to consider the time differences, and potential cultural differences (a topic we will touch upon in later chapters of our book), it is possible to have a meeting with a client in China and a client in Europe on the same day.

Virtual selling also gives you improved access to talent, which can improve your success rate in meetings. Previously, the people who could attend client meetings might have been limited by the geographical location of your team. In the virtual world this is no longer a problem. You have access to a global talent pool. That means you can introduce your customers to more members of your team who can demonstrate their expertise in a particular area. Having their input might help you make the sale. The customer will see that you can deliver on what you are promising. In our experience, you have an increased win rate when you can expose your customer to more than just your salesperson.

The other side of this is that you are able to gather the key decision makers into one meeting much more easily than in the past. Research has found that a typical business-to-business sales decision now involves an average of six to eight people.[5]

Virtual selling allows you to bring together all the people on your customer's side who you would like to be involved in the sales process.

Health and wellness

Employees who spend more than 21 nights in every six months travelling for work are more likely to:[6]

- Smoke
- Have trouble sleeping
- Be obese
- Have alcohol dependency
- Suffer from depression or anxiety

As you well know, when you travel a lot you spend a lot of time sitting down. You will eat unhealthy foods often at odd times of the day. It is difficult to maintain an active lifestyle. You are exposed to hundreds of people in airports, on planes, and on trains, and therefore the chances of you becoming sick are increased.

There is also the stress associated with travelling, with more than 60% of employees stating that they get stressed when they travel for business.[1] When you travel for work, you will potentially spend long periods of time away from your family and friends, and this can negatively impact your mental health. Changing to virtual selling could help you to address some of these issues and help you and your team have a better quality of life.

Benefits for your customers

There are two main ways in which virtual selling benefits your customers: providing more frequent touchpoints and health and safety, which is particularly important in a post–Covid-19 world.

More frequent touchpoints

When you have to travel to meet your customers, you are more inclined to organise meetings with them once every six months rather than once every month. When you have these six monthly catch-up meetings, they tend to be long. You have a long PowerPoint presentation to deliver, and you are presenting so much information that it can be overwhelming for your customer.

With virtual meetings, you can schedule more frequent touchpoints and make those meetings shorter. Instead of one long, bi-yearly meeting, you can have short monthly meetings to touch base. This has many benefits:

- Arrange the meetings for times that work for you and your customer, saving both of you time.
- Discuss what is important for that customer at that point in time—not what happened five months ago.
- Spend more time throughout the year interacting with your customers—having 45-minute meetings 12 times a year gives you double the time with your customer compared with three-hour meetings twice a year.
- Pivot and adjust your strategy based on what your customer needs.
- Improve agility to make decisions.

Having shorter and more frequent virtual meetings makes you more effective. Research shows that effectiveness drives high customer satisfaction.[7] As virtual meetings can make you more effective, they will lead to higher business impact for your customers and better results and can thus result in higher customer satisfaction.

Health and safety

The Covid-19 pandemic also means businesses have to consider the health and safety of their employees when they are hosting face-to-face meetings. Removing the need for you to travel to visit your customers' offices removes the chances that either of you could spread the virus. Some clients may even have policies that will not allow you to visit their offices. Giving your customers the choice of a virtual meeting is more important than ever in a post-Covid-19 world.

Remember that your clients will also be adapting their businesses to suit this new virtual-first model. As they become more accustomed to virtual sales methods and technologies, they will more easily and readily differentiate between organisations that run virtual sales meetings well and those that run them poorly. Taking the time to embrace virtual selling and hone your process now will mean that you are one step ahead of the competition in the months and years to come as virtual selling becomes more commonplace and more accepted among your clients.

Benefits for your company

There are three main ways in which virtual selling and working will benefit your company: reduced expenses, improved customer experience, and creation of a happier and healthier workforce.

Reduced expenses

The average business trip costs between $1,073 and $2,537 per person, per trip.[8] Commercial teams account for 80% of business travel and expense spending.[9] The same research also shows many businesses (70%) find it difficult to forecast their travel and expenses, while half of companies do not have full visibility of the return on investment (ROI) of their business travel costs. The virtual world presents many opportunities to not only reduce the amount you are spending on business travel but to also increase the revenue you generate from your most valuable clients by improving their experience.

Better results

As we discussed earlier, under the Benefits for you section, you will have more time to spend in meetings with customers when you work virtually. Our research found that, on average, salespeople can save 34 hours a month by converting physical meetings to virtual ones. For a company, this means more sales from more opportunities, as well as better conversion of those opportunities, by enabling experts in addition to your salesperson to interact with customers during the sales process.

34 Hours per month can be saved by converting physical meetings to virtual ones

Happier and healthier employees

When your sales team has a better work-life balance, better health, and are delivering the same or better results with less effort, this all leads to higher employee satisfaction. Happier, more satisfied employees are more productive, deliver better customer service, and are less likely to leave your business.[10]

Adopting a virtual sales model also allows you to have a more diverse salesforce at your company. Virtual working can bridge gaps in location and enable working parents to take roles they may not otherwise have considered. The more virtual you become, the less your company will be limited geographically when hiring new talent and the more attractive it will become for professionals in different stages of their personal and professional lives.

When you are working virtually, it can also help your teams to cross cultural divides because of the ability to interact more frequently not only within teams but across teams within the business. This creates a culture of inclusivity, which is particularly relevant for multinational businesses and companies that are seeking to increase their international presence.

The most attractive companies are moving toward a flexible working model, where employees can choose whether they work from home, from the office, or a combination of the two. Offering that flexibility will have a positive impact on how your brand is perceived as an employer.[11]

Benefits for the planet

Sustainability and reducing the environmental impact of your business are likely to be something you are already striving for. Reducing the amount that you and your team have to physically travel could have a significant positive impact on the planet and thereby the sustainability of your business.

Reduced CO_2 emissions

Did you know that business travel is responsible for an average of 50% of a business's carbon emissions?[12] Research conducted in the United States shows that before the Covid-19 pandemic, an average of 1.1 million people travelled by plane for business every day, emitting nearly two tons of carbon into the atmosphere.[13] When you sell virtually, you no longer need to fly or drive to meet your customers. This will significantly business CO_2 emissions.

Bringing innovative products to the world

Working and selling virtually presents opportunities for even small startups with limited travel budgets to reach marketplaces all over the world. There are many small companies that have great products and solutions that can help solve global issues.

In the past, reaching international marketplaces has been challenging, but the shift to virtual selling will enable small and medium-sized companies to access the entire world and share their sustainable solutions much more widely than before. Larger companies can benefit too, using virtual selling to more quickly prototype product ideas with a wider array of customers.

Give me the hard facts please!

Virtual customer engagement enables organisations to increase sales efficiency and effectiveness

Increased efficiency
– free up time for more and higher quality engagements

 20%
Less travelling provides more time (and saves costs)

 63%
Virtual meetings are shorter and more to the point

 60%
Physical meetings that can be converted to virtual

Increased effectiveness
– increase win rate and shorten sales cycle

 57%
Rethinking value messages and adapting presentations to a virtual format improves win rates

 40%
Easier access to more stakeholders shortens the sales cycle

 37%
Access to subject matter experts is likely to be better in the virtual environment

We conducted a survey of over 300 people in commercial executive positions across various industries between 22 June and 20 August 2020. This is what we found:

- 60% of existing customers are open to meeting virtually.
- 63% of people have found virtual meetings to be shorter and more to the point.

- 60% of the meetings we used to have physically can be converted to a virtual setting.

From a sales perspective, we uncovered some specific benefits to holding more meetings virtually:

- Salespeople save an average of 34 hours per month by converting physical meetings to virtual meetings.
- 40% agree that the sales cycle is shortened by going virtual due to easier access to key stakeholders.
- 57% agree that by adapting the form and content of sales presentations to suit a virtual format, the win rate is improved.

 IDEA IN *brief*

- Virtual selling has been accelerated by the Covid-19 crisis, and our research found that 70% of companies are likely to run virtual customer meetings in the future.
- The benefits of virtual selling range from benefits for you, for your customers, for your company, and for the planet.
- The reduced need of corporate travel allows you to free-up time, increase your productivity and boost your results, as well as have a positive impact on your health and wellness.
- Virtual selling also benefits your customers, by allowing for more frequent touchpoints to address real-time issues, and increased health and safety due to no face-to-face contact.
- A virtual sales model also has corporate benefits: reduced travel expenses, improved customer experience, happier and healthier employees.
- Virtual sales benefit our planet by reduced CO_2 emissions, reduced corporate travel and increased spread of innovation.

Overcoming the barriers

In the next chapter, we will explore the barriers that currently often prevent virtual meetings from being as effective as face-to-face meetings, and we will give you some tips and tricks to help you overcome these barriers.

Chapter 2:

OVERCOMING THE BARRIERS TO VIRTUAL CUSTOMER INTERACTION

Dealing with barriers in your meetings

Glancing at the clock on her computer, Kim could feel her stress levels spike. 9:57 am. She had turned on her computer, happy she would not have to show her messy face, bruised from this morning's fall, and proud to be logging in early to take a few moments to gather her thoughts before the call. Now, however, she could feel herself going into panic mode as she realised that the time was ticking until she would be expected to turn on the video camera.

I have to do something about this bump. Kim ran into the bathroom, desperately trying to fix her makeup to conceal the bump on her forehead. In her rush, she dropped her cosmetics bag, scattering makeup and brushes all over the floor. She cursed under her breath, reaching below her bathroom sink to retrieve her concealer. Just as her hand closed around it, she heard her living room clock chime 10:00 am. In a panic, she ran back to her computer, rushing to log into the Zoom meeting, and hoping Paul would join a few minutes past the hour.

As she frantically tried to log on, she realised her Internet connection wasn't working. *What do I do about that?!* It was 10:03 am, and she could feel her heart pounding and her blood pressure rising. Suddenly, she remembered one of her kids fiddling with the modem when he couldn't join an online computer game. She dashed upstairs to the bedroom, where she found that she'd pulled the modem out of the electricity socket when she'd fallen out of bed. She plugged it back in and waited just long enough to see the green light flash on. Sweat was dripping from her injured forehead.

Back at her computer, Kim finally connected to the Zoom call. It was 10:08 am and Paul was already waiting in the virtual meeting room, looking slightly irritated. "I'm so sorry I'm late," Kim started to say, only then realising that Paul could not hear her sound. *What else can go wrong on this call?!* she thought, desperately Googling how to turn on her sound. Eventually, she picked up her headset and could finally see Paul picking up what she said.

Kim could hear her voice trembling as she apologised again for being late, while browsing through her laptop to access the presentation file on her drive. Even through the screen, she could sense Paul's irritation grow with every second she was silently looking for her presentation. As she finally uploaded the file, she glanced at the clock in the corner of her screen. 10:16 am. She suddenly realised she only had 14 minutes remaining in her virtual meeting. *How am I going to make it through this deck? It will take me at least 20 minutes to walk through the contents of the proposal …*

She took a deep breath and began. Kim rushed through the slides, making sure to at least briefly cover every slide that was in her 89-slide presentation deck. Her gaze kept drifting to Paul's video in the corner of her screen, where she could see he was visibly disengaged. Paul was yawning, turning away from the video and answering text messages. Feeling even more distressed, Kim spoke faster still, struggling to keep the flow of her storyline. At slide 71, Paul interrupted her.

"Sorry Kim, but I actually have another meeting that started a minute ago, so I really need to drop off now. Perhaps we can reconnect another time?" Kim felt like she'd frozen in her tracks. A quick glance at the clock showed it was 10:31 am. "Sure, thanks a lot for your time Paul, and good luck with your next meeting," she heard herself say as Paul was exiting the virtual meeting room.

How do I come back from this? Kim thought, looking at her own disheartened expression staring back at her from the empty virtual meeting room.

The elephant in the virtual meeting room

Do Kim's challenges sound familiar? While Covid-19 accelerated the trend toward virtual sales, it is a trend that has been around for some time—in fact, up to 61% of sales meetings were already held over the phone or virtually even before the crisis.[1] So why is having an impactful, engaging, and effective virtual meeting so difficult? We believe the reason lies in two keywords: trust and engagement.

Trust is a precondition of a successful sales relationship—and for most of human history, we have developed trust with each other when interacting face-to-face. During 2020, the lion's share of human interaction turned virtual, taking away the physical element of our interactions that we consciously and subconsciously use to build relationships with each other. The rules of building trust in a virtual setting differ from the way we naturally build trust during face-to-face interactions—and the perceived level of trust is likely to drop by 83% when interacting virtually.[2]

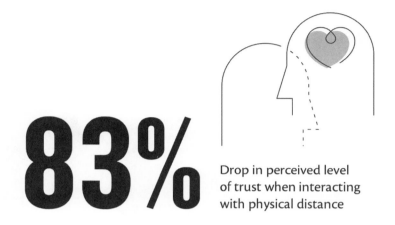

83%

Drop in perceived level
of trust when interacting
with physical distance

Engagement is another key element for effective virtual meetings. According to Harvard Business Review,[3] meetings typically have one of four purposes:

- To influence others
- To make decisions
- To solve problems
- To strengthen relationships

All of these are active processes that require *voluntary engagement*, hence passive participants are somewhat worthless. Virtual meetings are, by their nature, less likely to engage your audience compared to face-to-face interactions. In fact, studies show that over half of virtual meeting participants admit to multitasking during meetings; one in four participants plays video games and one in five participants is guilty of shopping online during virtual meetings.[4]

A lack of trust and engagement in virtual settings create four key barriers to effective virtual customer interactions: *physical, social, cultural,* and *technological.* We will explain why each of these areas is a barrier and then give you advice on how you can over-come each of them to improve your virtual customer interactions.

The Virtual Meetings Enemy #1:

DISENGAGEMENT

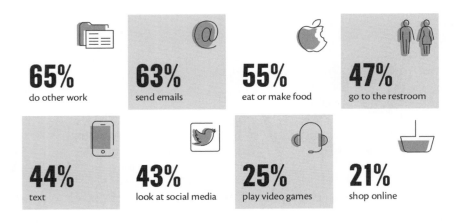

65%	**63%**	**55%**	**47%**
do other work	send emails	eat or make food	go to the restroom
44%	**43%**	**25%**	**21%**
text	look at social media	play video games	shop online

Survey by West Unified Communications Services in 2014 on 500 Americans

Physical barriers

Virtual interaction means we are physically separated and cannot easily decode each other's body language, especially if we do not have the video camera on during our virtual meeting. This presents a challenge as most of the information we gather from our interactions comes from nonverbal, rather than verbal, communication. This is rooted in our evolution. For many millennia, our feelings, emotions, and information were communicated primarily through body language, with spoken and written language only evolving around 50,000 to 150,000 years ago.[5]

Albert Mehrabian, often described as the father of the study of body language, found that only 7% of the impact of a message comes from the words we say (verbal communication), while 38% lies in our tone of voice (vocal communication) and 55% is shared nonverbally, through our body language. While the accuracy of these percentages has been the source of debate for many years, it is clear that we transmit, receive, and process information not just from *what* we say but also from *how* we say it.[6]

This effect is amplified in a business setting. When we do not know people well, we use nonverbal cues to understand them. In fact, body language accounts for between 60% and 80% of negotiation impact. It only takes 1/10 of a second to form a first impression,[7] and research suggests that body language enhances a "salesperson's charismatic appeal, which in turn leads to favourable attitudes towards the salesperson."[8] This can result in up to 25% more sales.[9]

Eye contact, facial expressions, posture, movements, hand gestures, and so on signal customer agreement or disagreement, engagement or disengagement. These nonverbal cues can give indications of questions, potential deep-dive points and buying interest. They can be a signal that you need to accelerate or slow down the agenda, all of which directly impact the outcome of the meeting.

Removing the ability to understand each other's body language in virtual interactions can therefore reduce trust, destroy engagement, and negatively impact the outcome of sales meetings.

What can we do to remove these barriers to our physical engagement with one another in a virtual setting?

Social barriers

Have you ever considered what difference it makes when you meet someone face-to-face as opposed to virtually? Humans are social animals. For thousands of years our survival depended on cooperation and belonging to a "pack." Our need for social interaction is so strong that our brain perceives a threat to our social connections in a similar way to physical pain.[10] Trust is a key precondition to building strong social bonds.

In the physical world we have natural social constructs to facilitate trust-building behaviours. We might kick off our face-to-face meetings with a trip to the coffee machine, a formal or informal round of introductions and casual conversations during breaks—all of which build social bonds resulting in a base level of trust. This trust is key for a successful relationship. Customers that trust you open up about their plans, share valued information, and purchase from you.[11]

Trust building does not come naturally in the virtual world. We have all probably been in a typical virtual meeting, where we connect a few minutes late due to a previous meeting running over, only for the meeting host to jump straight into the agenda and then have to recap the same points several times as people keep connecting over the course of the next few minutes.

The perceived level of trust is likely to drop by 83% when teams interact virtually versus physically.[12] This lack of trust results in disengagement and a hesitance to share information and ideas, which ultimately leads to a less impactful meeting.

How can we build trust in a virtual setting to enable us to conduct engaging, productive, and impactful virtual meetings?

Cultural barriers

Have you ever met a person whose approach was the exact opposite of yours? Someone you felt was too professional or too private? We have different standards and traditions for communication based on our cultural context, which can lead to misunderstandings, misalignment, and potential conflict. We are focusing on three key cultural aspects that are relevant in a customer setting:

- Background
- Personality
- Corporate differences

While you have to be sensitive to these cultural aspects in a physical setting too, they are amplified when we meet customers virtually due to the physical distance. This is why it is important to recognise, identify, and mitigate them if you want to host successful virtual meetings.

Background differences can create barriers if we are interacting with customers who come from a different background than ourselves. Eastern versus Western business cultures have significant differences in what is considered appropriate in corporate interaction—from differing levels of power distance to different ways of engagement and interaction. What is more, where multiple participants from different countries are present in virtual interactions, language can also become a barrier. Non-native speakers may potentially be less open to making spontaneous contributions.

How can we ensure that everyone, no matter their background, is comfortable and willing to contribute to the meeting?

Personality differences refer to the different modes of interaction and engagement that participants might display. Some people are naturally more extroverted and outspoken and might feel very comfortable navigating the virtual world, sharing viewpoints, asking questions, and engaging when they are interacting virtually. Others, however, might be more introverted and reluctant to share their inputs without being asked, preferring to formulate their thoughts before voicing them in an open meeting. Unfortunately, it is this latter group who can quickly find themselves at a disadvantage in the virtual setting.

Virtual meeting hosts often suffer from the fear of silence during virtual interactions. It refers to the lack of affirmation and two-way communication that is so often experienced during virtual interactions, particularly if the participants do not have their videos turned on and the host therefore is unable to see their reactions. This lack of feedback can cause hosts to rush through the contents of the meeting, or to overload the agenda to avoid uncomfortable moments of silence. The result is that the loudest and fastest voices are heard, and input from the more introverted participants is "lost in translation."

> Imagine if this more introverted participant is a key decision maker, influencer, or stakeholder. How likely will you be to move them along the sales funnel if you fail to activate and engage them during your virtual interaction?

Corporate culture differences can also create significant barriers in virtual interactions. When we meet customers physically, we are exposed to many cues for the accepted ways and standards of communicating within our customers' organisation. These range from their office space design to the dress code and style of interaction. Meeting customers virtually, particularly if they are working from home, prevents us from seamlessly gathering this information.

> How can we ensure that we have the required insight to address the customer in an appropriate and impactful way?

Technological barriers

Virtual interactions are powered by technology. We can probably relate to Kim's struggles with managing the technological element of virtual meetings. Most of us have probably experienced technological delays, disrupted meeting agendas due to technological troubleshooting and lagging virtual meetings.

Poor WiFi connection, sound or image issues, failing technology, meeting participants who lack technical skills, low-resolution images—the list of potential technology issues is endless.

Technology is unpredictable and, unfortunately, often fails us when we need it to run smoothly.

How can we reduce our technological risks to ensure we minimise potential disruptions?

The key barriers to effective virtual customer interaction

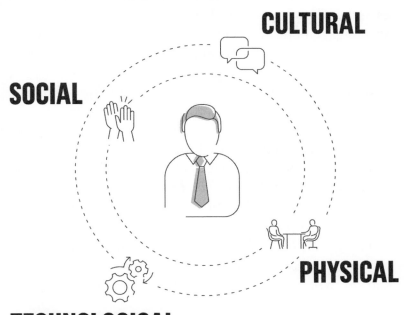

How to overcome these barriers to virtual success

Over the last six months, we have studied over 500 research papers, upskilled and trained over 1,000 salespeople across the globe in virtual sales, and gathered examples of best practice as well as the most frequently asked questions and challenges relating to overcoming these virtual barriers. We are going to share some of our key findings with you.

How to overcome physical barriers

These are the simplest ways to overcome the physical barriers you experience in virtual meetings because you and the other participants are in different spaces physically.

- **Turn on the camera:** This is virtual meeting 101. It is the easiest and most impactful solution to help you build trust and engagement. As soon as you turn on your camera you can see the person (or people) on the other end of the call. If the camera is correctly positioned, it can allow you to read body language and therefore accelerate trust building and engagement.

  Having your camera on mimics face-to-face interaction and can therefore make a virtual meeting feel a lot more like a face-to-face one. A top trick is to place a Post-It note with a smiley face on it to one side of the camera to remind you to smile. This will also direct your gaze toward the camera. This is especially important if you are using a platform where your on-screen video is positioned away from the camera. Set yourself up to actually look into the camera, and this will help build trust and engagement.

Mante's perspective

The meeting selfie

In one of our Virtual Customer Engagement training sessions, a participant asked, "But how do I overcome the physical barrier if my or my customers' bandwidth does not allow me to turn on my camera?" Another participant raised her 'virtual hand' to contribute with her perspective. She shared that many of her customers are based in remote parts of Africa, where bandwidth often is not strong enough to support a video call. She said that they often have virtual meetings via WhatsApp or just a simple phone call. In order to overcome the physical barrier without turning on the video camera, she always invites her meeting participants to share a "meeting selfie" with all meeting participants right before the meeting. While this still does not give her the opportunity to observe reactions and body language in "real time," it does serve the purpose of putting a face to the person on the other side of the line, thereby building trust among meeting participants.

- **Place the camera at eye level:** If the aim of using the camera is to mimic face-to-face interaction, then it matters how you are utilising the camera. It is very important that the camera is at eye level so that you are able to make eye contact with the person you are speaking to. Many of us use laptops, which often sit lower than our eye level and it can therefore seem as though you are looking down on the other person in the meeting. This could come across as condescending or threatening. A simple tip is to use a stack of books to elevate your laptop and bring it up to eye level for your meeting.
- **Show your body language:** By elevating your laptop or positioning your camera at eye level, you are also able to show your body language. This allows you to maximise your "virtual real estate." As we have discussed, body language is essential for communication, trust building, and engagement, so if you can share some of your body language it will help you get your message across more strongly.

  Consider using body language more than you would in a face-to-face meeting and accentuate it, because it does not come across naturally in a virtual setting if you do not consciously use it. Use your hands and make sure that they are in view of the camera to help show that you are open, for instance. This is all about building trust and engagement.

- **Do not restrict yourself to PowerPoint:** It is okay to come out of presentation mode and have more face-to-face contact in a virtual meeting. Do not feel forced to stick to PowerPoint. If you are dynamic in the physical world, you can be dynamic in the virtual world. It just requires preparation and thought. We will explore this more in Chapter 4.

- **Ensure your surroundings are fit for purpose:** Have good lighting, sound, and tech. Make sure that you are dressed for the occasion and that you feel confident. If you are working from home and feel that where you are working is not appropriate for your meeting, use technology to help you, for example, by using a virtual background.

  All of the main virtual meeting providers allow you to blur your background or offer virtual backgrounds. You can play around with your virtual backgrounds by having something professional behind you, like your latest launch or something you want to discuss during the sales call. You could also have a more personal background, like a holiday photo if that is appropriate, which can help with icebreaking at the start of a meeting.

- **Manage the energy:** It is important to remember that virtual is just the way that you are hosting the meeting—it is still a meeting. If you were hosting a physical meeting, you probably would not speak for 1.5 or 2 hours without having a break, interacting, or just standing up and stretching. The same rules apply in virtual meetings.

  If you have participants who are in different time zones where it might be morning for some people and evening for others, it is important to be aware of that and, as the host, to adjust accordingly to make sure the virtual meeting is a good experience for all. We plan our virtual workshops to include breaks, to allow for people's biological needs and give them time to get a coffee or a water. Playing music can also help with energy levels.

People's attention span is shorter in a virtual setting than in the physical, so we recommend planning a break every 30 minutes. During those short breaks, you can try to get that "coffee machine" talk going. Using a simple visual cue like a slide showing a cup of coffee can help encourage people to have a social discussion that is not necessarily related to the agenda, just as you would if you were in a physical setting. Interaction is key to breaking these barriers. You want to have a dialogue, not a monologue. We will cover these points in greater detail in Chapter 6.

Mante's perspective

Managing the energy across time zones

I ran a workshop recently where most of the participants were in the UK, but we also had two participants in Australia. In the beginning of the meeting I worked out that, for the Australian participants, it was close to midnight where they were based.

I simply made a point of asking them if they'd like to grab a coffee because they had two hours of the workshop ahead of them, and I knew it was close to midnight where they were. This put a smile on the Australian participants' faces—they really appreciated me being considerate. The other participants based in the UK had not been aware of the difference in time zone—so we all had a short laugh and celebrated the Australians' commitment to attending the session outside usual work hours. I could feel how this completely changed the atmosphere of our virtual interaction—all of a sudden, we felt like we were a team, like we were "in this together," although we had met for the first time. I could feel the trust level skyrocket.

Recognising things like this is important, as it not only makes you aware that people might have different energy levels, which will affect your meeting outcome; but it also allows you to build trust and engagement, which is a precondition for virtual meeting success.

How to overcome social barriers

As we said earlier in the chapter, in virtual meetings we do not have the same means of building trust and relationships with each other. However, there are ways to replicate these in the virtual world.

- **Virtual coffee machine:** In a normal face-to-face meeting, you would meet your customer in the lobby, welcome them, offer them a coffee and have a little chat before starting the meeting. This element of meetings can be very easily lost in a virtual setting, where the tendency is to jump straight into the agenda.

  The virtual coffee machine is a great trick to cater to our needs as social animals in the virtual. This involves inviting people to join the meeting five minutes early, and planning five minutes into the agenda, to break the ice, give people time to arrive, and to ask them how they are. It is important that you, as the host, facilitate this because it does not come naturally in a virtual setting.

- **Show a "sneak peek" of yourself:** Do not be afraid to show personal aspects of your life, especially if you are working from home. You are inviting people into your personal space, so you can position yourself strategically to share certain personal elements of your life, such as books on a shelf or family photos on the wall. You can design the corner of your home where you will be running your virtual meetings to share a certain message about you.

Another interesting perspective, which we learned from speaking to body language expert Marc Bowden, is that when you meet someone for the first time and you are doing it virtually, you are immediately very close, and perhaps even in their personal space. This accelerates the interaction from what you would experience in a face-to-face meeting, where you would shake hands and typically not see the other person as closely as you do in virtual meetings. If you are consciously aware of this, you can take advantage of it because it can help to accelerate trust building.

- **Embrace bloopers:** It is okay that not everything is perfect, because we are all in this together and this situation is new for your customers as much as it is new for you. When something goes a bit wrong, like your children interrupting or your cat appearing in your video, it shows your human side, which builds trust and helps people relate to you more easily.

- **"Take a risk" and share a personal story:** We relate to each other through personal stories, and sharing a little piece from your personal or professional life can make you more relatable in a virtual setting—hence, building trust between you and your customer.

- **Leverage technology:** You can create good energy using music, or you can use different apps to create engagement. Take full advantage of the fact that you are online to introduce different tools where it is purposeful. This technology does not only have to relate to conversations; it can allow you to conduct polls, make annotations, do drawings, and so on.

- **Brief introduction:** If there are many people in your meeting and you are limited on time, we recommend having a slide that says, "State your name, position/title/(use whatever is relevant for the meeting) in the chat function." Many people find this works well because it gives context about all the participants without taking up lots of time. Another of our top tips is to ask everyone to verbally introduce themselves in one breath. This is a great way of keeping verbal introductions short and sweet.

- **Address people by name:** This is important to create a quick connection. A simple tip is to have a printed list of names at hand to allow you to refer to people by name, because this creates trust and relation.

Christian's perspective

Using interruptions to your advantage

With more and more of us working from home, it can be challenging to create an entirely professional environment, especially if you have children. In the months that I've been working from home, I would estimate that my youngest child has "interrupted" 20% of my virtual interactions.

He's come in to give me a goodbye kiss, sit on my lap, whisper something in my ear. I could have decided that this was a problem and sent him away. Instead, I've chosen to embrace these interruptions. Sending my children out of the room would make me a worse version of myself and would play on my conscience. I'm also aware that people decide whether they trust me based on how I act toward someone else, including a child.

As you'll know if you have kids, these unforeseen interruptions will happen. You can't lock the door because then they'll just hammer on it until you let them in. If you embrace these events, you can use them to your advantage. I've been in virtual sessions where no one was really interacting in the chat, but as soon as my son came in, they started asking questions and making comments. People were smiling. These events introduce a human perspective and help to break the barrier.

It's the same when a child interrupts one of my customers. We'll smile, spend a couple of minutes talking about their kids, and that enables us to connect on a deeper level.

How to overcome cultural barriers

As we explained earlier in this chapter, cultural barriers can arise from differences in cultural backgrounds, locations, personality, and also corporate culture.

- **Take control as the facilitator:** It is important to be aware of these cultural differences that might be present, and as the host, it is your responsibility to ensure that everyone in the meeting feels comfortable and able to contribute. Guide the meeting and invite people to contribute. Be upfront about how and when people should and can contribute.

- **Design the meeting to fit with different personalities and cultures:** There are several elements to consider when designing your meeting. Be aware that some people will be open to jumping in with information or questions, while others will be more reserved. If you have participants who are not using their mother tongue, recognise that they might be reluctant to contribute or that they could struggle to understand the input.

To help overcome these barriers, design different ways of interacting. For example, you might invite people to contribute vocally or in the chat function. Remember that someone who is not that comfortable speaking English might be more comfortable writing it. In a sales context, it is really important to be aware of this.

In face-to-face meetings, it is often a case of the loudest voice wins. In the virtual world, however, you can introduce different modes of interaction, and this can allow you to gain perspectives that otherwise might not be heard.

As a facilitator, it can be easy to fear silence if you are not aware of this and to try to pack the space with words. However, it is important to create space for people who might not be comfortable with just blurting things out to share their input.

- **Align on "rules of interaction" to overcome cultural differences:** This links to the first point about taking control. Be upfront about how people can interact. Tell your participants if it is okay for them to interrupt to ask questions, or whether there will be a Q&A at the end.

  The aim is to remove any uncertainty or internal barriers someone might have about contributing, because in the virtual world it can be hard to read the cues you would have in a face-to-face setting.

- **Invite a co-facilitator:** Having a local co-facilitator can help you to mitigate risks associated with language barriers, as well as helping you increase engagement. This is particularly the case if there are lots of participants in the meeting. Ideally, find someone who can contribute value to the meeting beyond speaking another language. This makes it perfectly natural that they would be there as a co-facilitator. Introduce them as facilitation support or tech support so that all your participants understand their role.

- **Prepare in advance:** Do your research on who is joining the call—know their position, title, tenure, and any other relevant factors for your meeting. Also take the time to research the corporate culture of the company. Even without physical contact, you can find out a lot by visiting their website and reading annual reports and so on.
- **Be relatable:** Learn simple phrases in the local language to help create a connection with the people you are meeting. Also, do not underestimate the power of positive reinforcement (especially when dealing with cultures)—find ways of acknowledging people's input/contribution to the conversation, be it liking their comments in the chat or doing so vocally.

How to overcome technological barriers

Technology can be unpredictable, but there are several simple steps you can take to do your best to ensure your meetings run smoothly. You do not have to become a tech guru to overcome technological barriers.

- **Prepare!:** Make sure you have a plan B. Virtual meetings are powered by technology, and technology is unpredictable, so you cannot be 100% sure that something will not happen. The key is to try to anticipate what might happen. For example, your Internet connection could fail, so have a fully-charged mobile phone next to you that you could use as a personal hotspot. If the sound is not working, make sure you have the other person's mobile number so you can call them on the phone to have the audio and continue to share the visuals in your virtual meeting. Try to imagine all the technical things that could go wrong, and then come up with a plan to mitigate each one before the meeting.
- **Communicate tech requirements in advance:** Remember that your customer might not have the same technology

as you. Give them the chance to install the software, check with their IT department, and do things like get a camera if theirs is not working. Give them a head's up about what tech you will be using and what you expect from them. When you take the element of surprise out of it, it increases the likelihood that the technology will work as it should.

Also be aware of things like firewalls and how these could disrupt your virtual meeting. Test the specific features/functionalities you wish to use with people outside your own organisation ahead of time, ideally with a trusted sponsor from the organisation you will be working with.

- **Join in advance:** Do not keep your customer waiting in the waiting room. If you are going to have your five-minute virtual coffee machine before the meeting, then join 10 minutes before that to check that your sound, images, and everything else is working.

  A top tip is to use the virtual coffee machine to check that everyone's tech is working. If you do not have too many participants, directly address every person in the meeting, as this will help you identify whether any of them are having problems with their sound, and it is a chance to check that they can hear you. The other advantage to the virtual coffee machine is that if there are any issues, you have five minutes to solve them or mitigate them before you start your meeting.

- **Invite technical support:** Most salespeople are not IT gurus, so do not be afraid of inviting someone for tech support and advice. You could have a technical facilitator, or you could have someone from your IT department who is on standby to help you.

- **Have your materials on hand to share if you need to:** This comes back to being prepared, so think about all the technical things that could go wrong in your meeting and have a Plan B. Remember that even though the issues in tech might be quite advanced, the solutions can be very simple.

For example, if your video does not show because the Internet is poor, then have a link that you can post in the chat function so that people can watch it on their own. Or if your presentation does not upload, send your slides to your participants as a PDF and just talk them through which slide you are on as you deliver the presentation. Alternatively, if you have a technical facilitator on the call, then just ask them to share the slides so you can take control of the presentation.

- **Do dry runs:** Doing dry runs for important sessions is essential, and again, it links back in with being prepared. Tech issues will negatively affect your meeting engagement and energy, because they are annoying and waste precious time. Think about Kim's story that we shared at the beginning of the chapter. As a salesperson, tech issues also throw you off your game. As well as having to think about your storyline, being convincing, and managing negotiations, you then also have to think about tech. As we have already said, most salespeople are not tech gurus.

  Your dry run is also an opportunity for you to work out how you might switch between different materials or tools, for instance. It is all about preparation, which we will discuss in greater detail in Chapter 4.

  Doing a dry run will help you identify potential issues, and it will help you plan and prepare more effectively. Knowing that you have this plan in place in case something goes wrong will also give you more confidence in yourself during your virtual meeting, which in turn will improve the quality of your virtual meeting.

How to overcome virtual barriers *Checklist*

PHYSICAL

- Turn on your video camera
- Place the camera at eye level
- Do not restrict yourself to PPT
- Ensure fit-for-purpose surroundings
- Manage the energy

SOCIAL

- Invite for a "virtual coffee machine" talk
- Show a personal side of you
- Embrace bloopers
- Share a personal story
- Address people by name

CULTURAL

- Take control as the facilitator
- Design the meeting to fit different personalities and cultures
- Align on "rules of interaction"
- Prepare in advance
- Be relatable

TECHNOLOGICAL

- Prepare
- Communicate tech requirements in advance
- Join in advance
- Invite technical support
- Have a Plan B

FAQs: How to solve common queries

How do I get my customer to turn their camera on?

Inform them in advance that it will be a video meeting. Take the element of surprise out of the equation and thereby reduce the threat response.

What do I do if it is a hybrid meeting, with some participants joining virtually and some physically?

Generally, we find that to effectively host a meeting, it is best to choose one form—either physical or virtual. However, if some of your meeting participants are joining from their home office, while others are co-located, you can approach facilitating the meeting in several ways. You can ask the co-located participants to also join via their personal computers, so you have individual "virtual" eye contact with each of the participants. If this is not possible or suitable, you can ask the co-located participants to place the video camera in a way that will give you a full overview of all the participants. While not giving you access to individual micro-expressions, this will give you the opportunity to "read the room"—and when the co-located participants want to contribute, you can ask them to consciously speak into the camera, if the video-conferencing software does not automatically direct toward the speaker.

How do I manage the time spent during a roundtable introduction and ensure it isn't too long?

Invite everyone to introduce themselves in one breath—this helps to both keep the introduction time to a minimum and add a bit of positive, playful energy into your meeting.

If I have many people on the call, how do I remember everyone's name?

It helps to have a printed list of participants on hand when you run your virtual meeting.

What if I don't have time in the agenda to waste on ice-breaking activities?

Trust is key to a successful sales meeting, so ice-breaking activities are time well spent, as they help you establish this trust and engagement. Remember that these icebreakers do not have to be long, but dedicating just a few minutes at the start of your meeting to build trust will have a tremendous impact on how effective the meeting will be.

My meetings start hour to hour, so we can't invite people to join five minutes early.

The virtual coffee meeting should not be something you are forced to do, but still schedule it in the calendar. Inform the customer that it is voluntary to join. As it is a virtual coffee meeting, use it to create a good energy with music playing, rather than jumping straight into the meeting from a silent waiting room.

Inviting a co-facilitator just for language barriers might be perceived as a loss of face by my customers. How can I avoid that?

Try to find a role beyond the language facilitation for your co-facilitator. Perhaps you have a local expert available who could contribute interesting and valuable perspectives as well as providing local language capabilities? If they can add value beyond their language abilities, it will feel more natural for them to be there. Frame it to your customer that this person is helping to run the meeting.

I remember to ask questions during my virtual meetings, but the response is usually simply a "mute" line. How do I get my meeting participants to answer me?

In meetings with bigger groups, avoid asking open questions to all participants, as people are often less inclined to break the silence and be proactive. Ask specific questions to specific people and in this way ensure everyone has a chance to contribute to the conversation. If you feel that asking specific people might be perceived to be too direct, make sure to give them a head's up by letting people know in advance that you will be asking them for comments or reflections after you go through the specific topic.

It is usually the same people that are actively participating in customer meetings. How do I get everyone, including the ones that are silent, to participate, without being perceived as threatening?

Calling people out on the spot can indeed trigger a threat response. A way to ensure you get less-active participants to contribute vocally is by nudging them into participation. We usually give virtual meeting participants a head's up that we will be asking for their input by saying, *"We will ask for your comments and reflections, and we would like to hear from someone who has not yet voiced their opinion."* This creates a common understanding and expectation that we will be calling on people who have not been vocal yet, and thus is not perceived as threatening.

IDEA IN *brief*

- Even though virtual meetings have become common-place, it is very difficult to conduct meetings that are impactful, engaging and effective virtuallly.

- We believe the key reasons for why achieving a great virtual experience is so difficult are the lack of trust and engagement in the virtual setting.

- This creates four key barriers that are present in virtual meetings: physical, social, cultural and technological barriers.

- Understanding, addressing and overcoming these barriers are key to running an impactful virtual meeting that is also a great experience for you and your customer.

- In this chapter, we explore simple and hands-on tips and tricks for how you can effectively overcome virtual barriers.

Enhance interactions using the virtual world

In the next chapter, we are going to introduce you to the hybrid sales model and look at not only how virtual meetings can replace meetings you would have in the physical world, but also how you can use the virtual world to make those interactions even more valuable for your customers. The idea is to reinvent the sales process, not simply transfer what you do already in face-to-face meetings into the virtual realm.

Chapter 3:

THE HYBRID SALES MODEL

A second chance

Kim sat and stared at the empty screen for some time after the meeting ended, before finally turning away. Where had all the excitement she started the day with gone? She sighed, feeling as though she might cry.

I made so many mistakes! How can I ever come back from this? Although the meeting hadn't gone well, Kim decided to turn to her solution-mindset and find a way to win the deal, despite the disastrous meeting in the morning. She refilled her water glass, sat at her laptop and tried to concentrate.

A few hours later, her phone pinged. It was a message from Paul. Kim could feel her excitement return. She took a deep breath and decisively tapped her phone screen, the words flashing up in front of her.

"Hi Kim, I know the meeting this morning didn't go as you'd planned and I recognise that putting you in the position of having to deliver your presentation virtually at the last minute meant you didn't come across as you normally do.

It felt as though the virtual environment was new to you, and I actually had a similar experience in my first virtual meeting, so I'd like to suggest we give it another go. One of your competitors brought a product expert to the meeting. I'd like to schedule a new meeting with you and give you a chance to do the same. Paul"

Kim exhaled in relief. *I haven't blown this. I will make sure I nail the next virtual meeting.* A smile started to creep across Kim's face. She tapped a response out to Paul.

"Thank you so much Paul, I really appreciate this. I will contact our product experts to check their availability in the coming days. I look forward to speaking again soon. Kim"

She saw Paul replying. His message simply read, "Thursday would work for me if at all possible." *Right, I've got some organising to do.*

Kim picked up her phone and called Eric, the top product expert and internal sales trainer at the company. She knew he was usually busy and travelling a lot, but she hoped he might have a bit more time at the moment. Kim was amazed when he answered after just one ring—she'd been expecting to leave a message and hear back from him later.

After a bit of small talk, Kim briefly outlined the meeting that morning, referring to "technological issues" rather than going into the specifics of her morning from hell.

"What do you think? Do you have time to do this meeting with me on Thursday?" Kim concluded.

"I have time on Thursday, a lot of my customer visits have been cancelled so I'm quite flexible the next few weeks. I think we have quite a bit we need to talk about though. What's the exact purpose of this meeting?"

"The purpose … ?" Kim said hesitantly, even though she had been expecting questions because she knew Eric liked to plan every detail of a meeting.

"Yes," Eric responded. "What do you want to achieve in this meeting, and what are the steps that are going to get us there?"

Kim paused. She'd always considered herself to be someone who performs at their best when they improvise and aren't constrained by a detailed plan.

"The purpose is to win this business," Kim said, more confidently.

"That might be the eventual outcome, but that's not the purpose of this particular meeting. We have to think more strategically, about what we want from the next meeting and the one after that," Eric replied. "Wasn't it you who once told me that we don't just meet people once and seal the deal?"

Kim had to admit he was right. In the past, when she'd brought Eric into meetings, they'd been much more successful at onboarding clients, but she always had several meetings after his initial involvement before they signed on the dotted line.

Am I going to have to do all of these meetings virtually? Kim thought, feeling the panic begin to rise again. *I'm not sure I'm cut out for this.*

"This could be a great opportunity," she could hear Eric saying. "There is so much we can do virtually with clients that's tough to do in a face-to-face meeting. Let's catch up tomorrow to put a plan in place."

"Okay, that sounds good," Kim said, with as much enthusiasm as she could. *This is not how I normally do things, although I'm pleased Eric seems to have a better idea of how to handle virtual meetings than I do. I do wish he'd go with the flow a bit more, though. I always feel so constrained by a detailed plan. With support this time, maybe things will go better. Maybe I can turn this around with Paul …*

Virtual sales: An opportunity for improvement

Kim's colleague Eric has a fair point. A meeting is not just a meeting, and you need to align your meeting design (whether virtual or face-to-face) to best deliver on that objective. If you involve other people in your meeting, it is advisable to have a plan to help divide responsibilities and avoid getting off track.

This was true in the face-to-face world and it is even more important in a virtual setting, where you are less likely to have the time/energy/skill to do a lot of improvisation during the meeting. It is very important to remember that going virtual is not just about converting your old ways of working to virtual platforms.

There are two common perspectives surrounding virtual sales. One is that you just use virtual to replace what you used to do before. We consider this to be the "brain friendly" approach. The brain is designed to save energy, and for that simple reason, we want to go back to "normal." However, there is no guarantee that what used to be normal will become the new normal.

Our research revealed that 60% of salespeople expect to conduct a higher proportion of their future customer/sales meetings virtually compared to the time pre-Covid. The same percentage of customers are open to virtual meetings in place of face-to-face ones. This means that if you expect to get fully back to what was the normal way of working, you could fall behind your competitors and disappoint some of your customers.

The other is that you use the best of the virtual environment to reinvent your interactions with your customers and make them even more valuable than before. This perspective is not as "brain friendly," but it is much more likely to lead to success in the future.

Instead of asking the question, "How do I conduct my traditional meetings virtually?" you should ask another question: "How can I improve the quality and frequency of customer or prospect interactions by combining the best of face-to-face and virtual meetings?" We call this the hybrid sales model, which will not be 100% virtual or 100% face-to-face, but a combination of the two. There are several situations where it is possible to make a situation better than it was before by using virtual interactions. Let's look at three of the most common.

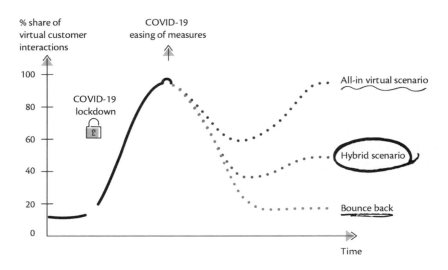

Multiple decision makers

One example is where there are multiple decision makers involved. In the business-to-business buying process, research has shown there are typically between six and eight people[1] involved in making the decision, and if you are only having face-to-face interactions it can be very difficult to get access to all of these people, for various reasons. They might be in different locations, it might be hard to get your calendars to match, or maybe your contact person does not want to put you in front of a senior decision maker.

As a salesperson, you are taught that the more decision makers you can meet and make your advocates, the more likely you are to win the deal. However, when our prime model of interaction is face-to-face, we often struggle to get access to all of these people for the reasons mentioned above.

Virtual meetings could overcome some of these barriers if they are used and organised correctly. It is generally much easier to involve these people virtually than it is to get them to all come together for a face-to-face meeting. For instance, if it is impossible to get all six decision makers in one room to facilitate a consensus, invite them to a joint 30-minute virtual meeting that no one has to travel to.

If meeting all of them together is not possible, ask your contact for permission to host a short, 20-minute virtual interview with each stakeholder to ensure all of their perspectives are included. The main advantage to virtual is that these meetings can be shorter and do not require any travel time.

Bringing in your busy expert

Another example is where you are able to bring in an expert, who would normally be too busy to physically travel to meetings. There is a lot of research to show that customers prefer to meet an expert, because everything they can learn from a standard salesperson is online or in the brochure. As a result, they value expert advice much more. Research from CSO Insights[2] found that less than one-quarter (23%) of buyers named vendor salespeople as a top three resource to solve business problems.

Forty-three percent of the same buyers selected industry experts as a top resource. Consider the implications of this! If you can position your experts to customers, you are more likely to be involved in the solution design and therefore have the opportunity to influence the solution, build a relationship with the problem owner (rather than only having to deal with procurement), and effectively position your differentiators.

However, in most commercial organisations, experts are a scarce resource. There are generally not that many of them, and those that do work in a business are often travelling, which means they are unable to join your sales meetings. Virtual presents a huge opportunity here. You can get your expert to join your meeting virtually, even if you are meeting your client face-to-face. Our research found that 37% of organisations believe that access to subject matter experts is better in the virtual environment.

Christian's perspective

Improving service with virtual interactions

One of our client's sales director is an expert on logistics, and due to the Covid-19 pandemic, he ended up having a virtual meeting with one of the company's regional customers who would normally only deal with the local salesperson.

After the sales director had that call with the customer, the customer got in touch with him to suggest a change to the structure of the regular meetings. Instead of having eight meetings a year with their local salesperson, this customer said they would prefer to have four virtual meetings a year with him, the logistics expert.

The customer wanted to replace some of the face-to-face meetings with the local representative with fully virtual interactions with the sales director because what they got out of that call was what they needed to develop their business. The customer recognised that they needed to interact with someone like the sales director to move their business forward. The difference in the content they got out of the meeting with the sales director compared with a meeting of their local salesperson was significant.

The point is that when this sales director has more time because he is not travelling so much, he is able to serve more customers as an expert. This is the kind of scenario you can take advantage of with a hybrid sales model.

How does your role change in a hybrid model?

Virtual customer meetings are a way to help you get in contact with even more customers in the short term. However, the real opportunity lies in setting yourself up for greater success from your meetings.

When the Covid-19 pandemic hit, all of a sudden it was not possible to visit your customers anymore. The first line of defence was to meet them virtually. When we talk about the advantages in the short term, this is what we mean. Virtual tools have allowed you to meet with customers you would normally see face to face, but who, due to travel restrictions, you are no longer able to meet with in person. For many people, virtual is just seen as a way of getting in touch with their customers.

However, if you think about virtual in the long term, you will start to see how you can use it to become more successful, just like the examples we provided above. There are many other scenarios where virtual interactions can be beneficial.

For example, you could have a short, 20-minute virtual interaction with your customer before you go to a sales meeting. This will give you an opportunity to tell them what three topics you are planning to talk about and ask if any of them are more important than the others. If you do this virtually, you can better prepare for your meeting and focus on the topic that your customer is most interested in, rather than spending 45 minutes presenting equally on all the topics only to discover it was topic number three that they were really interested in. In this example, you are looking for new ways you can interact with your customers to enhance what you already do.

It is also important to note that if virtual allows you to connect more people to your customer, then your role changes a little bit. It is not necessarily you who has to turn up to the meeting and know everything.

For instance, you could call in your supply chain manager when you are talking about how you will set up deliveries, or you can bring in your quality expert. When you think of virtual as your tool as a salesperson to connect your customers with more people from your organisation, you become more of a facilitator, rather than someone who has to explain what you are doing in every area, whether that is quality, the supply chain, or somewhere else. The point is you do not have to know it all; you simply need to know who the right people to connect are.

You also have to explore how the virtual world allows you to have a higher number of more relevant interactions. For instance, one of the customers we work with has a lot of big existing customers. Twice a year, they go to them and have a full-day meeting where they discuss big agendas with long PowerPoint presentations. We are pretty sure everybody in those meetings is bored, but because they travel so far, they feel obliged to spend a full day on this meeting.

Consider what it would mean if, instead of having this long and boring meeting twice a year, you had more frequent but shorter meetings. This would mean that you are more relevant, more up to date with your customer's concerns, and that you are able to find out about the problems and issues as they occur, instead of half a year later when they have grown so big that the customer is really annoyed.

This is where we feel the role of the virtual has the potential to change the role of the salesperson. If you, as a salesperson, embrace the virtual, it can actually be a new way of connecting people and facilitating the exchange of information and inspiration.

A sales meeting is not just a sales meeting

As Eric pointed out in his call with Kim, when a customer goes through a buying process you will meet them on several occasions. There is no such thing as just one type of sales meeting.

A sales meeting could be any of the following scenarios (and plenty more besides):

- *Inspiration meeting:* Meeting with someone who is not yet a customer for the first time where you want to inspire them to start considering buying from you.
- *Request for proposal (RFP) meeting:* Meeting with an existing customer to discuss whether you can deliver what they need.
- *Demo meeting:* Meeting to run a demo of your company's product or service.
- *Negotiation meeting:* Meeting to negotiate with your customer about specific points.

Each of these different meetings, or interactions, will have a different objective. As a result, you need to be aware that your preparation and the way you conduct your virtual meeting will be different in each of these situations.

One virtual way of doing things does not fit all meetings, so you need to consider the purpose of your interactions and then design your virtual meeting accordingly. We will explore how you can best prepare for your virtual meeting in Chapter 4.

Exploring the different virtual interactions in the sales process

Let's look in greater detail at some of the different virtual interactions we listed above, and what your objective might be in each.

Inspiration meetings

This is where you want to inspire a customer or potential customer to start considering their needs and to consider talking to you about your product or solution. The objective of this meeting is to get someone to consider having a dialogue with you about your product. The following is a very simple example, but it illustrates what we are talking about clearly.

Imagine you receive a phone call from an insurance salesperson. They say, "Hi sir, is this an inconvenient time? I'm from XYZ insurance company and I wanted to know if you would be interested in buying insurance?"

Your response here will be "No, I'm not interested" because you are not in the process of buying insurance and you probably already have insurance.

A more effective way to approach this interaction would be to start the call with, "Hi sir, I'm AB from XYZ insurance company. We have learned that, on average, we can save people up to 30% of their insurance costs. Would you be interested in seeing if that applies to you?"

You can see the difference in those two approaches, and we are sure you can see which will be the more effective interaction in terms of getting potential customers to talk to you.

If we take that idea and put it into a business-to-business (B2B) context, what you have to do is go to a meeting with a new potential customer and show them how your company has helped another organisation that is similar to theirs achieve a specific business outcome. You are inspiring them and giving them the potential to improve. However, if you turn up and just tell them that you have a really great product that you think they need without linking it to their specific situation, they are far less likely to engage, especially if they already have a similar product with a different company.

So, how do you get a potential customer to consider having that dialogue with you after a virtual inspiration meeting? Firstly, you have to be a really good storyteller. You only have a few seconds to get them hooked. This kind of meeting does not work well with lots of slides. You quickly need to show them which other types of organisations have benefited from working with your product and what value they have obtained as a result.

RFP (request for proposal) meeting

An RFP meeting is where a client has approached you and asked for a quote for your services or product. If we go back to our insurance example, the buyer will already be in the process of buying new insurance. They have already carried out research and created a specification for the type of insurance they want and the value it has to cover. At this point, the buyer might contact five insurance companies and ask them to provide quotes based on this specification.

If you are a salesperson in this kind of meeting, you do not want to start trying to inspire them to change insurance by sharing the business value you brought to another organisation. You do not need to convince them that they should consider changing insurance because they are in the process of doing so. In this meeting you will have a different objective, which is to show the customer that you can deliver on their needs.

In an RFP meeting, you should also try to show a customer how your product is better than those of your competitors, because if they are hearing pitches from several companies and you are all pretty much equal, it is likely to come down to price. You have to demonstrate that they get more value for money with your product than they would get elsewhere.

Let's just take a moment to compare how your role as a salesperson would vary between an inspiration meeting and an RFP meeting. These two virtual meetings will look very different. In the inspiration meeting, you as the salesperson will take the lead. In the RFP meeting, it might be that the customer takes the lead by presenting their needs to you. The same approach and presentation do not fit both of these types of meeting.

Demo meeting

When you have a demo meeting, it is likely that you are further down the sales process with a customer. Maybe you have convinced them that they need to do something through your inspiration meeting, and then your customer issued an RFP to several different vendors. This is where the customer says to you, "Show me your product."

If you are in the physical world and you have a physical product, then they can touch it, they can see it, and they can see how it works. However, if you cannot meet your customer in person, you still need to give them a feel for your product. Getting a feel for a product is often an emotional process, and it can be challenging to make that emotional impression virtually.

As a salesperson, just showing a picture of a product and talking through a PowerPoint is unlikely to create an emotional impression with a customer. However, if you can show them and talk them through how the product works, that can help. When you are conducting virtual demos, you need to prepare in a different way than how you would for, say, an inspiration meeting.

You have to consider how you can charge your customer's emotions if they cannot physically touch the product you are showing them. For example, rather than you telling the customer how fantastic your product is, could you invite one of your existing customers to share their experiences and tell your new customer how they have been using your product?

You do not necessarily have to bring an existing customer into the meeting. It might be that you video some testimonials with your happy existing customers that you can use in any demo meeting. Or you could share pictures or videos that show how another customer is using the product. For this demo meeting to have that character and to create that sense of emotion, you need to prepare properly.

Negotiation meeting

A negotiation meeting will typically happen toward the end of the sales process, and this is where, if you meet face to face, you will be seeing the person responsible for purchasing or procurement. Typically (although not always), there will be a lot of tactics involved in these kinds of meetings.

If you are one of, say, three people from your company who is involved in the negotiation meeting, you need to have a plan about how you will approach it and who will speak when. For example, the customer might say, "You're 30% more expensive than the next placed alternative. What are you going to do about it?"

In a physical meeting, you can look at one another and see from each other's body language who should speak and who should be quiet. In a virtual setting you will not have those cues, so you need to prepare beforehand to ensure you are all on the same page.

For instance, if you are expecting a hard negotiation, maybe you agree that in the middle of the meeting you will have a 10-minute break, where you can talk to your two colleagues and agree on a response, rather than one of you just jumping in without consulting the others. Or you can take advantage of technology and share a separate platform outside of the virtual meeting room with your colleagues, where you can align on next steps and negotiation tactics.

These are just four examples to show you how a virtual version of a meeting can be different to a physical version of that same meeting. The point is that virtual meetings can have different requirements due to the fact that you are physically distant from the other participants. It is therefore important to understand that you have to prepare for them differently than how you would prepare for a physical version of that meeting.

Exploring different virtual interactions with your existing customers

Sales is not only about attracting new customers; it is also about providing a good service to your existing customers to ensure that they remain customers with your business. There are various kinds of meetings you can have with your existing customers. We are going to look at just three examples here.

Business development meeting

This is a meeting where you would ask your customer to share their strategy and long-term plans with you, because if you have a better understanding of this you will be better placed to advise them on how your company can help with their strategy.

You might have solutions in your portfolio that will be helpful to your customer, but to suggest the right ones you want to take a longer-term look at your customer's business rather than just checking in to see how things are going. The objective for this meeting is to understand where your customer is going and identify potential opportunities for you to work together in the future.

If you host this kind of meeting face-to-face, you will more than likely have some informal dialogue around the coffee machine. If you are going to run a business development meeting virtually, it is advisable to ask your customer to prepare a brief outline of their strategy beforehand.

We already know that hosting meetings virtually can take away some of the trust between you and your customers, so you may need to be clearer when defining the objective of this meeting with your customer to ensure that it is successful.

Joint optimisation meeting

This is where you meet an existing customer to have a discussion about how you can improve the way you work together to benefit both of you. The objective here is to identify these ways of working that could benefit both of you and improve your interactions going forward.

For instance, you might approach your customer and say, "We've noticed that you seem to be ordering at this frequency, can you explain why that is, because we have inefficiencies on our side when we have to process fast deliveries on such a short timescale." Your customer's response might be, "That's because our long-term planning system isn't very efficient." At this point, you could have a conversation about managing their inventory for them, so that they do not have to manually place an order every time they need something, because you would be able to monitor their stock levels.

If you are having this as a physical meeting, you might want to bring in your supply chain expert or quality manager, and your customer might want to do the same. If you are doing this virtually, however, you might not want to cover all of this in one meeting. In that scenario, you could connect your quality manager with your customer's quality manager, and the same for the supply chain managers. That would allow you to have a higher number of shorter meetings that are more focused on a specific topic, rather than bringing together lots of people into one large meeting. This just demonstrates, once again, how virtual meetings can have a different flavour to physical ones.

Value capture meeting

These are meetings you have with your customer on an ongoing basis (we would recommend either quarterly or bi-annually) to discuss what value you have delivered to them during that period. It could be that you have helped optimise their supply chain through the joint inventory model we talked about earlier, or maybe you helped them sort out a quality issue quickly.

The reason you have these meetings, and gather this information, is that (and this is a very simplified example) typically, every three years, someone from purchasing at your customer's business will suggest that they try to get a 10% discount on the price of your services as a supplier. At that point, someone from procurement will contact you and tell you that they have five other alternative suppliers lined up to help them squeeze this 10% margin out of you.

However, if you have been having regular value capture meetings with your client for the duration of their contract, it puts you in a much better position when you have to negotiate with their procurement team. You will be able to document all the value you have added, and then you can say to them, "Ok, if we give you the 10% discount, which of these value-added elements should we take out of the equation?"

When you look at how you would approach this in the physical versus the virtual world, you might only have one value capture meeting a year, if at all, if you are doing everything face-to-face. However, if you do this in the virtual world you can arrange a monthly call for just 20 minutes with the supply chain manager where you can ask, "How did we perform this month? What kind of improvement initiatives should we put in place? What did you see from the improvements we carried out in the last month?"

This interaction does not have to be a big thing. The virtual equivalent is very different to the face-to-face equivalent, and the virtual interaction opens up more opportunities because you are able to do it more frequently, you can keep the meeting shorter, and you can do it with fewer people in the room and less traveling.

This ties back in with what we talked about in Chapter 1 in relation to having more frequent touchpoints with your customers and how this enables you to operate using the latest information.

The point of looking at these different types of interaction, and how you can use them in the virtual world as opposed to the physical, is to help you understand that by adopting this hybrid model and embracing the virtual way of working, you will open up new opportunities that improve the interactions you have with your customers.

IDEA IN *brief*

- 60% of salespeople and their customers expect to conduct a higher proportion of their future customer/sales meetings virtually compared to the time pre-Covid–indicating that virtual customer interactions are here to stay.

- We believe this presents an opportunity to use the best of the virtual environment to make your customer interactions even more valuable than before–we call this the hybrid sales model.

- The hybrid sales model will combine physical and virtual customer interactions also in the future, taking advantage of the best of both modes of interaction.

- Virtual interactions can help you engage multiple decision makers more effectively, scale your expert knowledge, increase the frequency of your existing customer interactions and free-up time for attracting new customers.

- Leveraging the benefits of virtual interactions also implies changes in the role of the salesperson toward connecting people and facilitating the exchange of information and inspiration.

- The benefit of virtual interactions will differ depending on the type of sales meeting, and we explore several types of sales meetings (such as inspiration, RFP [Request for Proposal], demo, negotiation meetings) and how virtual interactions can benefit you in these meetings.

Preparing for your virtual meeting

In the next chapter, we are going to explore how you can best prepare for the different kinds of virtual meetings you will hold. We have shown you how you can be innovative as a salesperson in terms of how you use the virtual world to interact with your clients, but it is important to remember that your preparation will depend on the objective you set for your meeting.

Chapter 4:

PREPARING FOR AN EFFECTIVE VIRTUAL SALES MEETING

Bringing in the expert

Kim sat at her kitchen counter, nervously tapping her finger on the side. She was clock watching and trying to calm down before the meeting. *It'll be okay this time. You're prepared.* She had already checked that her modem was plugged in, twice. She'd given herself time to put makeup on to conceal the now purple bruise on her forehead, and she'd arranged for the kids to spend an extra night with their dad to give her some peace and quiet.

She closed her eyes and took a deep breath in, letting it out slowly. *You've got this.* Her eyes flicked to the clock in the corner of her screen. She'd agreed with Eric that they'd both join the online meeting 10 minutes early to run through any last points. She loaded up the presentation that the two of them had spent the previous morning preparing, and she double-checked that she had her notes at hand.

As Kim logged into the Zoom meeting, she felt much calmer than she had just two days ago when she'd been in such a state trying to hold her meeting with Paul. She still wasn't comfortable in a virtual environment, but at least this time she didn't feel quite so much like a fish out of water.

She found Eric waiting for her in the meeting room. "Morning Kim," he said, beaming. "Are you ready for this?"

Kim couldn't help but smile back. "As ready as I'll ever be, I think!"

"Great. You're clear where you're going to hand over to me in the presentation?" Eric asked.

"Yep, I'll pass to you on Slide 27, and then I'll pick back up on Slide 40," Kim said, suddenly feeling a little more confident.

Eric smiled, "Great. I'll stay in the meeting but I won't jump back in unless you ask me to, okay?" Kim nodded and then saw that Paul was in the waiting room for the meeting already. *He's early!* Kim could feel herself starting to tense up, so she took one final deep breath before admitting Paul to the meeting.

"Morning Paul, thank you so much for making time to join us today," Kim said, forcing her best smile. "I'd like to introduce Eric. He's our product expert, and he'll be helping me with the presentation today."

She paused. Paul smiled. "Morning, Kim, and nice to meet you, Eric. I'm looking forward to hearing what you have to say."

"Great, let's get started," Kim said, sounding much more confident. She clicked into the presentation and started running through her slides, getting into her flow and improvising a little as she went. *This feels better*. Once she handed over to Eric, she relaxed a little, took a sip of water, and glanced at her notes to make sure she knew where she was going next.

Eric was sharing some interesting points about the product that she hadn't included. She quickly jotted down a note to refer to them toward the end of her presentation. She stole a quick glance at Paul in the corner of her screen. He was watching intently, occasionally making notes, but he appeared to be giving Eric his full concentration.

Kim prepared herself to pick back up and continue with the presentation. By the time she reached her final slide, relief was flooding through her body. Her smile was genuine as she said, "Do you have any questions for us, Paul?"

He smiled back. "There was just one point I wanted to ask about," he said, before querying one of the more technical details of the product. As Kim was listening to the question, she thought *How am I going to answer that?* Suddenly, she remembered Eric. She glanced at his image in the corner of her screen. As Paul finished his question, Kim said, "I'll let Eric answer that one for you." Eric took his cue and provided a very detailed answer. Kim could see Paul nodding and making more notes. *Thank God Eric was here for that!*

As Kim left the virtual meeting room, she was smiling. *That went well, didn't it?* She stood to make herself a cup of coffee, trying to work out whether Paul really had been impressed. *It's so hard to read people in these virtual meetings. I honestly can't tell if that was good. Paul seemed more interested than last time ...* Her thoughts were interrupted by a "Beep!" from her phone.

She reached across the counter to pick up her phone. It was a message from Paul. Suddenly she felt sick as she tapped the screen to open the message.

"Thanks for your time today, Kim. I really appreciated how seamlessly you and Eric interacted. I would go so far as to say that was the best prepared presentation I've seen so far. I do have one more pitch to see, but I'll be in touch soon. Paul."

Kim almost jumped for joy as relief flooded her body. A huge grin spread across her face as she tapped a quick response to Paul and then forwarded his message to Eric with the caption, "We smashed it!"

Why is preparation important for a virtual meeting?

While preparation is key for any sales meeting—irrespective of mode of interaction—many salespeople typically like to keep a certain level of flexibility and freedom in an agenda, to be able to adjust on the spot and shift the meeting focus to what appears to resonate the most with the customer and to capitalise on their personal charisma. Moreover, many can probably identify with the situation when you had to "wing it" and improvise on the spot to ensure you reached your meeting goal. Unfortunately, "winging it" is a hard quest in a virtual sales meeting—to reach your goals virtually, preparation is key.

The overarching reason why it is so important to prepare for virtual meetings is that it is very difficult to improvise in a virtual setting. It is something of a paradox, because in order to successfully improvise you need to prepare. There are three main reasons why it is challenging to improvise in a virtual setting:

- Their static nature
- Their complexity
- The challenges associated with creating engagement and building trust

The static nature of virtual meetings

Virtual meetings are, by their nature, more static than face-to-face interactions. You find yourself in a small virtual box in the corner and that limits your body language, takes away some of your freedom to express yourself and limits your personal impact as a salesperson. As a result, the sales presentation and pitch itself becomes the star of the show, taking up most of the "virtual real estate"—the lion's share of the screen.

The complexity of virtual meetings

When you are in a face-to-face meeting, you can focus solely on winning over your customer. However, in a virtual meeting you will have to consider the barriers we covered in Chapter 2, as well as managing secondary elements like technology, engagement, and making your customer feel good about the situation that you both are in.

With all of these additional things to think about, it can throw you off your game, especially if something goes wrong. Essentially, what this means is that you need an additional skill set when you are running virtual sales meetings. You are no longer just a salesperson, you are also a facilitator.

Disengagement in virtual meetings

As we mentioned in Chapter 2, building trust and securing engagement is key for developing relationships with your clients that will lead to successful sales meetings. It can be much easier for people to disengage in a virtual setting, so you have to be aware of this and manage it in your virtual meetings.

Our calendars are now so full of virtual meetings that Zoom fatigue is a real issue. We are sure you have experienced horrible virtual meetings at some point. The key is to prepare a meeting that turns our interactions from energy draining to energy giving.

The paradox of preparation and improvisation

Even if you are very experienced and very good at what you do, things are different in virtual meetings. If things do not go as you had planned, it can prevent you from performing to the best of your abilities. This is what happened to Kim at the start of our story—when her lack of conscious preparation resulted in a poor virtual meeting. The paradox is that, to ensure you are confident in your virtual meeting and to give you the ability to improvise, you need to thoroughly prepare for your virtual meetings.

The building blocks of virtual meeting preparation

Preparation is key in any type and mode of customer meeting, but in a virtual setting it becomes even more important because of the reasons we just outlined. It is important to understand that the way you prepare for virtual meetings has a twist to it.

There are three key building blocks to preparing for virtual meetings:

- Defining the objective
- Preparing an agenda
- Activating the audience before the meeting

Defining the objective

Every meeting, virtual or face-to-face, will have an objective. The twist in virtual meetings is that the objective will help define your guiding star for the meeting and keep you on track, even if something goes wrong.

For example, if your tech fails and you find yourself in a situation where you only have 10 minutes instead of 30 minutes for your meeting, you have to ensure that you achieve your objective within those 10 minutes. If you are not crystal clear on what it is that you need to achieve, you have no chance of figuring out how to deliver your message in an impactful way.

There are three questions you should be able to answer if you have prepared your meeting thoroughly:

1. **Objective:** What is the expected outcome of the meeting?
2. **Actions:** What actions are necessary to get the expected outcomes (e.g. develop, identify, prioritise, plan)?

3. **Qualifiers:** What important parameters/enablers do you have for your objective (e.g. time frame, top three priorities)?

OBJECTIVE ⇨ If you are well prepared for the meeting, you should be able to answer the following questions:

1 OBJECTIVE of the meeting
What is the expected outcome of the meeting?

Fill in here

2 Concrete ACTIONS during the meeting
What actions are necessary to get to the expected outcome?
E.g. develop, identify, prioritise, plan …

Fill in here

3 QUALIFIERS for the objective
What important parameters / enablers do we have for our objective?
E.g. timeframe, top 3 priorities …

Fill in here

Preparing an agenda

You will have an agenda for every meeting, whether virtual or face-to-face. However, the twist in preparing an agenda for virtual meetings is in time allocation. In a face-to-face setting, you will have some breathing time before and after, whereas virtual meetings are held within a set time frame and have a hard stop.

Due to the complexity of virtual meetings and all the elements you have to manage, you have to be very detailed about the time you allocate to each part of your agenda. Time allocation is the most important part of this step, especially as we usually underestimate the time things will take when we run virtual meetings. As a result, we have a tendency to over-stuff our agendas.

While there are some virtual meetings that might be quicker than face-to-face interactions, as we discussed in Chapter 3, there are other types of meetings that will take longer in a virtual format than they do in a face-to-face setting. These are typically meetings that involve co-creation and discussion. Generally, we underestimate how much time we need for these kinds of sessions in the virtual world.

In addition, facilitators often tend to be afraid of silence, which means they try to fill every moment of silence with words. As we explained in Chapter 2, this is not the best way to run a meeting. It is important to factor in some breathing room for your participants into your agenda, because some people might need time to reflect before they can share or contribute. This includes preparing the engagement and micro involvements to ensure that you have dialogue in your virtual meetings and not just a monologue.

Activating the audience before the meeting

The key point in activating the audience is to prepare your virtual meeting so that it starts before you have your participants in the virtual meeting room. We recommend that you do this by sending your participants a pre-read. This will achieve several objectives.

Firstly, it will help you overcome some of the barriers we discussed in Chapter 2 and will help you start to build trust. Secondly, you will be minimising the technology risks because you can tell people what technology you will be using in advance, as well as sharing expectations like making sure everyone has their camera on, and some of the other aspects we touched on in Chapter 2.

Thirdly, sending a pre-read is an excellent way to outline what you will talk about and get the customer's thought process started. Finally, it will signal that you are a professional salesperson and that you are preparing for this meeting.

Another important point to note in terms of activating your audience before the meeting is that if you are going for a face-to-face meeting and you have to drive for two hours to get there, the customer will be committed to the meeting because you are travelling to meet them.

However, when you translate face-to-face meetings into virtual meetings, that commitment can sometimes be lacking. This is because many people do not understand the amount of preparation it takes to run a virtual meeting. By putting together a pre-read and sending this to your customer before your meeting to activate their engagement, you can gain a greater level of commitment from them because you are showing them that you are having to do just as much work to prepare for this virtual meeting as you would if you were meeting physically.

A monologue is not a meeting

If you find yourself delivering a monologue, you are almost certainly not running an engaging meeting. A meeting, by its definition, involves two people and that means you want to encourage dialogue. As we just mentioned, you want to activate your participants before they join your meeting.

As well as sending a pre-read, you can ask people to prepare a small contribution for the meeting, whether that is outlining their priorities for you or giving you an overview of their company or a business issue they are facing. The important thing is that your participants know that they will need to contribute during the meeting, because this means they will not turn up expecting to play a passive role.

In that same email, you can also set the expectations for the meeting, such as having your camera on, maybe making sure they have a notepad and pen handy and so on. All of these small cues will tell them that they are going to be playing an active role and therefore will help them to engage before they join your virtual meeting.

Preparation sheet for your next virtual meeting:

AGENDA

Example for how a planned agenda and preparation sheet for a
60-min Customer Inspiration Meeting could look like:

TIME	WHAT	HOW	MICRO-INVOLVEMENT
-0:05 −0:00 before the meeting	Virtual Coffee Warm-up	How have you been since the last time we talked?	Opener: Round-table
0:00 −0:05	Framing the meeting	Purpose (objective), planned agenda, "rules of engagement", expected outcome	Check-in: *Do you agree on these suggestions? Is there anything you would like to add to today's agenda?*
0:05 −0:30	Presentation of key trends	Let people know in advance you will ask them to prioritise trends after the presentation; 10 min presentation of trends; 5 min reflection; 10 min presentation of remaining trends	5 min Check-in: *How do the trends presented resonate with you? Chat & voice over*
0:30 −0:40	Prioritisation of trends	Which of the presented trends do you believe present the greatest opportunity for your company and why?	Check-in: Poll, Chat and voice over – deep-dive on the *why*
0:40 −0:45	Confirmation of prioritised trends and impact case	Confirm prioritised trend and show brief impact case example where you succeeded in implementation	Check-in: *Do you agree that X presents the biggest opportunity for you?*
0:45 −0:50	Customer commitment	Ask for commitment from the customer to come back with detailed proposal	Check-in: *Can we come back with a proposal on how you can leverage this trend? / What would it take for you to be interested in us coming back with ... ?*
0:50 −0:55	Alignment of next steps & booking next meeting	Agree on the way forward, who will be responsible and next meeting date & participants	Recap: *We have agreed to ... to be completed by ... and we will reconnect on ...*
0:55 −1:00	Closure of the meeting	Ensure no misunderstandings / questions remain	Closer: *Is there anything that you would like to add?*

TO-DO LIST:

BEFORE MEETING
- Define and align on the meeting objective
- Prepare agenda, micro-involvements and pre-read
- Send welcome e-mail to participants with pre-read – incl. meeting purpose, agenda, preparations and technology required
- Invite participants to log in 5 min before
- Test technology in advance and log in 10 min before to test if everything is working well

DURING MEETING
- Turn on the video, smile and build trust
- Remember to ensure dialogue – engage participants
- Embrace it in case something does not go as planned and adjust based on your end objective – we are all human
- Make sure to effectively close the meeting and secure there are no misalignments

AFTER MEETING
- Send follow-up mail with summary of key points and actions discussed
- Invite for input / confirmation
- Involve customer in co-creation of the next meeting

IDEA IN *brief*

- Preparation is key in any meeting – but becomes particularly important in a virtual setting as it is very difficult to improvise.

- Improvising in virtual meetings is difficult due to their static nature, complexity and the challenges associated with creating engagement and building trust virtually.

- The key building blocks of preparing for a virtual meeting include defining the meeting objective, preparing the virtual meeting agenda and activating the audience before the virtual meeting to secure commitment, buy-in and engagement.

Capture your audience with strong virtual storytelling and presentations

In the next chapter, we are going to dive into virtual storytelling and explore how you can create engaging, impactful, and captivating virtual presentations. This is essential for success in your virtual sales meetings. Once you have addressed the four key barriers that are present in a virtual setting, it is time to look at the concrete tools and strategies you can use to create more impactful virtual sales meetings.

Chapter 5:

BUILDING ENGAGING VIRTUAL SALES MEETING STORYLINES AND PRESENTATIONS

Death by PowerPoint

The success of her meeting with Paul and Eric gave Kim a big confidence boost in the virtual world. Her next big test would be that afternoon. There was one item highlighted in her calendar for the day, a one-hour initial pitch meeting with what could be a big new client. Rather than feeling sick to her stomach about hosting this meeting virtually, Kim felt almost excited.

While she drank her coffee in the morning, she checked through her meticulously prepared PowerPoint. *I'm turning into Eric,* she thought with a smile. She knew it was a long presentation, but it needed to be to get all the information across. She had one eye on the clock all morning.

At 1.45 pm, she logged into the Zoom meeting, opened her presentation, and waited for her customers to arrive. There were 15 of them in total. As Kim shared her screen and launched into her presentation, she felt suddenly alone. *I can only see a few of them on my screen, I wish I could see how all of them are reacting ...*

Her presentation was going to plan, and she'd been talking for about 15 minutes when she glanced at the small thumbnails in the corner of her screen. *Not again,* she thought as she noticed that at least two of them were looking at their phones. Her heart started to race as she thought back to that first disastrous meeting with Paul. *What am I going to do?* She had reached the part of her presentation where she planned to talk about all the benefits of the solution when she remembered a meeting she sat in on with a colleague last week. He shared a story about one of their other customers rather than lots of slides. *I wonder ...*

Before she could lose her nerve, Kim stopped sharing her presentation and went back to a full gallery view, where she could see all the participants in the meeting. "I'm sorry that I've been talking at you for the last 20 minutes, I feel as though I'm boring you, so I thought I'd jump out of my PowerPoint for a short while to share a story with you," she said.

Kim subconsciously inched a little closer to her camera, noticing that several of the participants had stopped glancing at their phones and were now looking straight at her. She settled in, bringing her hands into a bridge in front of her and started to share the case study. *I love this kind of improvisation, even if my stomach is doing backflips!*

By the time she was half a minute in, she noticed that everyone was actively listening to her speak. She was enjoying being able to see everyone's videos too.

As she closed the story, her contact said, "That's very exciting, we had no idea you could achieve such impressive results in such a short space of time." Kim beamed. Everyone was smiling back at her. Having spent so long preparing her PowerPoint, she realised she could skip to the final 10 slides and round the pitch off there.

"Yes, it's really incredible what you can do with this solution. If you don't mind, I'd just like to jump back to my PowerPoint briefly for a few more slides, but then we can discuss this further before the meeting ends." Everyone was nodding enthusiastically. Kim felt a wave of excitement as she started to share her screen again. She scrolled to the relevant slides and ran through just five more. Her final slide said, somewhat drearily, "Thank you for listening." She chose not to display it, instead ending her screen share and going back to the gallery view.

"My question for you now is, what are the next actions we can take to move things forward?" There was a bubble of chatter at the question, and Kim felt pleased.

As she ended the meeting 20 minutes later, she had an actionable list of things both for her to do and for her prospective client to do, as well as a follow-up meeting booked in for the following week.

Kim sat back in her chair, allowing herself to relax now that the meeting had ended. As she took a sip of water, she opened her calendar to look at what else she had coming up. *I think I need to change my other PowerPoints for my sales pitches later in the week*, she reflected.

Creating impact:
The key to a successful meeting

Getting a virtual meeting with your customer in the calendar is only half the battle. Now you have to prepare to ensure that your meeting is a success. How do you do that in a virtual setting? How can you capture your customer's attention, help them understand and resonate with your content, and achieve the objective of your meeting? What steps can you take to ensure your virtual meeting has a lasting and tangible impact on the participants?

These are all questions we are going to answer in this chapter. We talked extensively about the barriers to engagement in virtual meetings in Chapter 2. Now we are going to provide you with concrete tools and strategies that you can use and build on to deliver more engaging virtual meetings that resonate with your customers, provide a better customer experience, and result in your meeting having the desired impact.

In our experience, virtual storytelling and strong virtual presentations are key enablers that lead to positive virtual sales impact.

What are the main challenges to creating impact in a virtual sales meeting?

When you are delivering sales meetings in a virtual environment, the challenges you face to driving successful meeting outcomes multiply. In addition to the physical, cultural, social, and technological barriers we have already talked about, there are four other challenges to be aware of.

Body language

As we explained in Chapter 2, body language is one of the key ways that we communicate as humans. You will be aware that you can use your body language strategically to strengthen a point, be more convincing, indicate agreement or disagreement, or show that you have questions. In a virtual setting, your ability to use body language strategically is limited because your screen "real estate" is often reduced to a small square in the corner of the screen.

Attention

When you meet in person, you can use your charisma to capture your customer's attention. In the virtual world, you are competing with a highly distracting screen environment. In a survey of 500 Americans,[1] more than 60% of virtual meeting participants admitted to being disengaged in a virtual setting, highlighting just how challenging it is to engage with your customer and retain their attention.

PowerPoint is the default

During great in-person meetings, your PowerPoint presentation is merely a backdrop for a fruitful in-person conversation. When we meet in virtual environments, we tend to default to our PowerPoint slide decks without considering whether this is the most appropriate way to engage our customers.

While a PowerPoint presentation can help facilitate and structure the discussion, it also takes center stage in a virtual environment and captures most of the participants' attention. This further exacerbates the lack of virtual "real estate" you have to enhance your virtual presence and creates a barrier between you and your customers. Look at how the dynamic of Kim's meeting changed as soon as she switched off her PowerPoint.

Memory

We have a limited attention span and tend to remember information selectively. For example, within 48 hours, your customers will only remember 10% of what you told them. How can you make that 10% count in a virtual environment?

The key to overcoming each of these challenges lies in impactful virtual storytelling and effective presentations. These are usually characterised by the following five elements (the Five Cs):

1. Connect to the participants
2. Catch attention

3. Content and conversations
4. Create understanding
5. Call to action

What makes a great story?

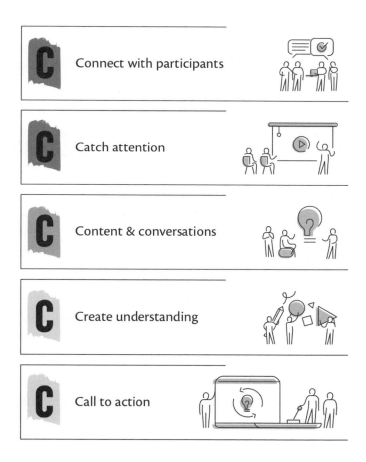

Connect to the participants

"A good start is half the battle", or so the saying goes. In the world of virtual sales, building an authentic connection with the participants in your meeting can get you off to a good start. In Chapter 7, we will discuss the importance of trust in virtual settings in more detail and give you advice on how to build it, but in terms of creating impact, a base level of trust is only part of the picture. Once you have this, how can you ensure you connect with your customers on a more fundamental level? The answer is storytelling.

The power of storytelling

Humans love stories. Stories are how we relate to each other, build trust with one another, and understand each other. There is a reason why we have chosen to start every chapter in this book with a short story about Kim—we wanted to have a colorful and relatable character who was facing the same challenges as us to exemplify the key points and concepts we are discussing throughout the book. By reading about Kim, we not only gain a better understanding of the challenges, benefits, and different situations, but we are also more likely to remember the key concepts better.

To understand why storytelling is so important and why we connect so well with it, we need to look deep into human history. In his book *Sapiens*, historian Yuval Harari explains that, biologically, there is no apparent reason why we as human beings took over the world. We are not stronger, faster, or otherwise physically superior to other animals. He argues that humans' power lies in storytelling.

Storytelling certainly has evolutionary importance. This skill has enabled us to collaborate in large numbers, develop trust with strangers, share visions and dreams, and persuade others. This is why we, as humans, continue to respond so strongly to stories and why they resonate with us on such a deep level.

Let's bring this back to virtual sales and how storytelling can have an impact on your meetings. You can leverage storytelling to capture and engage your audience, deliver your message in a more compelling way, and break down virtual barriers by connecting with your participants.

To do this effectively, you need a presentation that is much more than simply a list of bullet points. It should be a compelling visual and vocal narrative designed to showcase your products and services and how they deliver unique value. Great stories resonate with your customers because they show that you understand their needs and pain points. Often, the best stories are personal because they help your customer to relate to and trust you.

Mante's perspective

At Implement Consulting Group, we start each financial year with an Implement University. We invite global thought leaders to this event to inspire and challenge us. It's usually a three-day affair with 800 management consultants camping in the woods on a remote Swedish island, swimming in the sea, and having long conversations around a bonfire.

However, in 2020 we quickly realised that 800 people camping together on an island was not an option, and we needed to rethink our university concept. We decided to practice what we preach and took the event fully virtual.

- One of our keynote speakers in 2020 was world-renowned speechwriter Simon Lancaster. He talked about the cornerstones of building a great story, and he talked about three types of stories that can prove very powerful in both a general sales and a virtual sales context. They are:
- Metaphorical stories – "From darkness to light," "From troubled waters to safer shores," "From defeat to victory"

- Historical stories – "Putting a man on the moon," "The burning platform," "David and Goliath"
- Personal stories – "Last week, one of my clients called me and said something I'll never forget as long as I live ..."
- He also talked about different rhetorical devices that you can use to give your story more oomph—breathless sentences, exaggeration, and the rule of three.

Christian's perspective

I often begin my meetings by telling a personal story. There are several reasons why I do this. The first is that I'm super confident in my own stories. That means that when I start with a personal story, I'm starting my meeting from a place of high confidence, regardless of what we're going to talk about. When I begin my meeting from a place of such high confidence, it helps other people—my customers—to have confidence in me.

The second reason I like to lead with a story in virtual meetings is that I believe people connect with a person rather than with what you're saying. When you're trying to build trust and develop a relationship, you need people to connect with you as a person before they'll connect to anything else. In sharing a personal story or anecdote, you're showing who you are and creating that personal connection.

The final reason is that it often surprises people. Sharing a personal story is not necessarily what people expect from someone in my position as a consultant. By disrupting people's expectations, you capture their attention much faster.

Catch attention

A catch is a word, sign, or slogan that is designed to capture the attention and stimulate the interest of your audience. As Christian mentioned in his story, often that involves doing something unexpected.

How to build a strong catch

Being able to capture your audience from the moment they log in is key to creating impact in your virtual sales meeting. There are three steps that we recommend following to build a strong catch:

1. **Know your audience:** A strong catch will only succeed in capturing your audience's attention if it is relevant to them and resonates with them. This means you have to understand and know your audience to help you build a strong catch. This includes knowing their profiles, pain points, aspirations, and targets.
2. **Do the unexpected:** A strong catch challenges your customer's thinking, brings up new or different perspectives, or adds new knowledge or value to the conversation. Consider what your audience might not expect to hear and/or see in your presentation.
3. **Keep the end in mind:** Make it easy for your customer to understand and remember your points by creating a "closed loop" in their mind. This means that you connect your catch and the follow-up to what you want to achieve in the meeting, the content you are sharing during the meeting, and the next steps you want to take with your customer.

How to build a strong catch?

1

Before you start, make sure you **know your audience**

2

Catch and stimulate the interest of the audience by **doing the unexpected**

3

Keep **the end in mind** – create a "closed" loop in the mind of the audience

Example

- What is the meeting objective?

- Who is my audience?

- What type of sales meeting am I having?

- What value has your customer not yet considered?

- What may your customer not yet know that could be interesting?

- What does your customer expect you to do in this meeting?

- What do you want to achieve in this meeting?

- How will your catch be supported by the content of the meeting?

- What will be your next steps that you expect to align on with the customer?

Questions to help you build your catch

We suggest that you begin by asking yourself three simple questions relating to each of the three steps for building a strong catch:
Know your audience

1. Who is my audience?
2. What type of sales meeting am I having?
3. What is the meeting objective?

Do the unexpected

1. What does my customer expect me to do in this meeting?
2. What might my customer not know yet and find interesting?
3. What value has my customer not yet considered?

Keep the end in mind

1. What do I wish to achieve during the meeting?
2. How will my catch be supported by the content I share during the meeting?
3. What are the next steps that I expect to agree with my customer?

Tips and tricks to create a good catch

 *Tips & tricks*
To make a good catch

 Make a bold statement or series of statements

 Ask a question

 Use a quote

 Make a prediction

 Show a video

 Tell a story

Have a clear OBJECTIVE

Know your AUDIENCE

Keep CONTEXT in mind

Whatever catch you create, make sure that you have a clear objective, know your audience, and keep the context in mind. Here are some tips and tricks to help you create a good catch:

- Make a bold statement, or series of statements—for example, "Most companies in your line of business can reduce their administrative cost by up to 18%, by applying our workforce planning solution."
- Ask a question—for example, "What would be the implications for your business, if your competitors suddenly reduced their administrative costs by 18% and reduced their end user prices accordingly?"
- Use a quote—for example, "Reducing our administrative costs by 18% allowed us to reduce end user prices and gain a 6% market share increase, as reported by Person X from Company Y."
- Make a prediction—for example, "Within the next two years, most insurance companies will have reduced administrative costs by up to 18%, and as a result end user prices will be reduced by up to 8%."
- Show a video—for example, you can show a video where a reference customer of yours tells and shows how they have reduced their administrative costs and how they have used this saving to either increase margins or gain market share.
- Tell a story—for example, "We recently worked for another insurance company. Their CFO was looking for ways to reduce their admin costs by 10%, so they could become more competitive with their end user prices. We delivered

such a solution, and as a result, today their admin costs are 6%-point below competitor index and they have gained an 8% market share increase."

Key questions to help you understand your audience

If you are struggling to pin down who your audience is, ask yourself the following questions to help you with your preparation:

- What type of sales meeting are you having?
- What is the purpose for this group (your audience) coming together?
- What are the current business issues facing this audience/organisation?
- What job responsibilities/roles/titles does your audience have?
- What does the audience want to hear from you?
- What problem are you helping the audience address?
- What is the desired outcome from this presentation?
- Where is the audience in their buying process?
- What presentation techniques can you use to engage your audience?

KEY QUESTIONS TO HELP YOU UNDERSTAND YOUR AUDIENCE

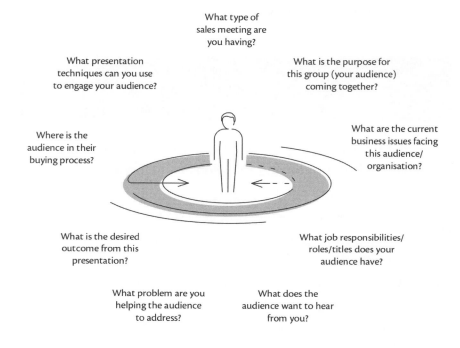

What type of
sales meeting are
you having?

What presentation
techniques can you use
to engage your audience?

What is the purpose for
this group (your audience)
coming together?

Where is the
audience in their
buying process?

What are the current
business issues facing
this audience/
organisation?

What is the desired
outcome from this
presentation?

What job responsibilities/
roles/titles does your
audience have?

What problem are you
helping the audience
to address?

What does the
audience want to hear
from you?

Content and conversations

One big idea

"I didn't have time to write a short letter, so I wrote a long
one instead"

– Mark Twain

This famous quote from Mark Twain illustrates how difficult
it is to present content in a concise form. To be persuasive,
engaging, and memorable in our virtual sales meetings, we need
to understand the way our brain works.

Most of our decision making is automatic and impulse driven,[2] which means it can be predicted. Therefore, if you can predict how your customer will react to your content, you can account and prepare for it.

The content for your meeting should be based on ONE BIG IDEA. This is the key element that you want your customer to take away from your storyline. Recall from previous chapters that we only remember 10% of what we hear in meetings[3]—this big idea should be your 10%.

Once you have your big idea, use three to four supporting facts to reinforce it. Use different techniques, such as storytelling, visuals, and conversation, to get your supporting facts across to the audience. Remember to sum up after each supporting fact to make sure that you and your audience are in sync.

It is also important to understand why you need to take control of your content. As we mentioned earlier, within 48 hours of your meeting your customers will only remember 10% of what you told them. If you do not take control of what you want them to remember from your virtual sales meeting then it will be susceptible to random memory.

Use visuals

Using different techniques for sharing your content, and particularly your BIG IDEA, is important, but sharing information in a visual format is especially vital. This is because 83% of the information we take in comes from our eyes, so to make your BIG IDEA come across, back it up with simple visuals (pictures, quotes, videos, etc.).[4]

Content and conversation

We have already explored storytelling and explained that it is a powerful tool for you to use because it is relatable for your customers. The other element that should form part of your meeting is conversation. We know that two-way conversations help to "sync" our brains in a process known as neural coupling.[5]

When we are involved in a dialogue, as opposed to just listening to a monologue, our brain releases endorphins (happy hormones). When you create this dialogue with your customer and give them the opportunity to be part of a meaningful conversation, you create engagement and encourage agreement.

"88% of decision makers want to have a conversation, not a presentation or sales pitch."

– Forrester Research

The content of a good presentation should invite conversation and encourage everyone in the meeting to feel involved in what is happening. You are turning them into active participants rather than passive listeners.

One simple way to ensure more conversation in your meetings is to prepare the questions you would like your customer to reflect upon, and tactically embed these questions into your presentation flow. A good rule of thumb: For every three slides or five minutes of your presentation, ask your customer a minimum of one question to spark a dialogue.

Questions to help you create your content

- What is the key message you want to convey?
- What is the one thing you want your audience to remember?
- What message will help you drive impact/achieve your objective?

- What facts support your big idea?
- How can you convey those facts in an interesting way? (Consider using videos, pictures etc.)
- Is there a clear connection between your supporting fact and the big idea?
- Are you summing up after each fact to repeat/control focus toward the big idea?
- What questions will get your prospective customer involved in the presentation?

 How to build content & conversations centered around one big idea?

| Center the content around one **BIG** idea | Use 3-4 **supporting facts** to reinforce your idea | Sum-up after each supporting fact to ensure **you are in sync** |

Example

- What is the key message you want to convey?

- What is the thing you want your audience to remember?

- What message will help you drive impact / achieve your objective?

- What facts support your big idea?

- How can you convey those facts in an interesting way (consider pictures, videos, etc.)?

- Is there a clear connection between your supporting fact and the big idea?

- Are you summing up after each fact to repeat / control focus toward the big idea?

Create understanding

This links in with both your content and your call to action, but you want to ensure that your customer understands your pitch and what will happen next.

To create understanding, you want to focus on one big idea, as we have already discussed. At the end of your presentation, restate your big idea and tie this back into your catch. Remember you are creating that "closed loop" in the mind of your participants. Often people will remember the catch from the meeting, so by leaving them with a clear link between your catch and your big idea, you are creating understanding.

Let's explore how this could look: **Catch** -> **Big idea** -> **Conversation** -> **Create understanding:**

Catch: "We recently worked for another insurance company. Their CFO was looking for ways to reduce their admin costs by 10%, so they could become more competitive with their end user prices. We delivered such a solution and, as a result, today their admin costs are 6%-point below competitor index and they have gained an 8% market share increase."

Big idea: "Within the next two years, most insurance companies will have reduced their administrative costs by up to 18%, and as a result end user prices will be reduced by up to 6%."

Conversation: "What would be the implications to your business, if your competitors suddenly reduced their administrative costs by 18% and reduced their end user prices accordingly?"

"What would you be able to do with an 18% reduction in admin costs?"

"What market share gain would you win if you reduced your admin costs ahead of your competition?"

Create understanding: "What I wanted to share with you today was the fact that **(BIG IDEA)** within the next two years, most insurance companies will have reduced their administrative costs by up to 18%, and as a result end user prices will be reduced up to 6%. If we tie that back to my initial story **(CATCH)** of how another insurance company gained an 8% market share increase by reducing their admin costs, there is strong evidence that being among the first movers to reduce admin costs can lead to quite a significant market share gain.

Call to action

You can keep the call to action in your virtual meetings very simple by ending with the next steps and making plans for those next steps to take place. If you think about the typical closing slide to a PowerPoint presentation, it will say something along the lines of "Thank you for listening." Instead, your final slide or your call to action should be a question:

What do we do now to take this one step further?

Ending your meeting with an action-driven question will encourage both you and your participants to consider the transition to the next stage of the process. You can make this even more powerful by asking the customer for their perspective and input on what those next steps should be. When you involve them in this decision, they are much more likely to commit to that next action.

Top tip: Make your final slide an action-driven question to your customer, rather than a summary of your presentation.

Tips and tricks for PowerPoint presentations

- Make your presentation visual because pictures are easier to understand than words.
- Add illustrations to your text to increase understanding (Levie and Lentz).
- Think of your PowerPoint slide as a billboard: Its message must be processed in less than three seconds (Duarte 140).
- People learn better from words and pictures than from words alone (Mayer).
- Words and pictures work best when they are presented near each other rather than farther away, and simultaneously rather than successively (Mayer).
- Use a mix of essential keywords and content-related messages (Mayer).
- Do not add images for decorative purposes only (brand content aside) (Mayer).

Why be visual?

There are many compelling reasons to make your presentation visual. As the saying goes, "A picture says more than a thousand words."

- Our brains respond most strongly to the visual sense.[6]
- Processing what you see takes up about half the resources of your brain.[7]
- Studies show that people pay attention to movement in the visual field.[8]
- The more visual your presentation is, the more memorable it will be.[9]
- It only takes the brain a bit more than **1/100 of a second** to process an image,[10] but it takes an average of six seconds to read 20 to 25 words.[11]
- Presentations using visual aids are 43% more persuasive than those without.[12]

The key is to plan time in at the end of your presentation to have this conversation and shape the next steps with your customer.

IDEA IN *brief*

- Virtual storytelling and strong virtual presentations are key enablers that lead to positive sales impact - especially given the challenges associated with virtual sales meetings.

- The main challenges to creating impact in a virtual sales meeting are the lack of ability to use body language, difficulties to keep customer attention, PowerPoint presentations often becoming the default engagement option and limited attention span.

- Virtual storytelling and strong virtual presentations are key to overcome these challenges and consist of five key elements (5C's): Connect, Catch, Content & Conversations, Create, and Call to action.

Engaging your customers virtually is key

In the next chapter, we will take a deep dive into engagement with your customers in a virtual environment. As we mentioned in Chapter 2, it can be challenging to build engagement in a virtual setting. We will share advice on how you can do this effectively to take your virtual sales meetings to the next level.

Chapter 6:

EFFECTIVE VIRTUAL CUSTOMER ENGAGEMENT

Is anyone listening to me?

Just two days after her successful sales meeting, where her storytelling had really captured the attention of her prospects, Kim once again felt deflated. She had just finished her second big pitch meeting of the week, and it couldn't have been more different.

As Kim hit the "Leave meeting" button on her screen, she felt a wave of relief that at least the meeting was over. *That was such hard work!* Despite delivering a much shorter presentation and telling her story like she had in her other sales meeting earlier in the week, she had still struggled to keep people interested.

Every time she had glanced at the thumbnails in the bottom corner of her screen it seemed like the participants were doing something else—she could tell a couple of them were on their phones for most of her presentation, and she was sure she'd seen one guy eating a sandwich at one point. Kim sighed; she felt disheartened.

I've been getting so much better at these virtual meetings, what did I do wrong today? Kim didn't have time to worry about that, though, as she had a follow-up call with another client just 15 minutes later, giving her just enough time to grab a coffee and pop to the bathroom.

As the end of the day rolled around, Kim was still thinking about her late morning meeting. *I can't put my finger on where it went wrong.* She was replaying it step by step in her mind and getting increasingly frustrated as she walked to collect the kids from school. She felt guilty that she was so distracted the whole way home, but she couldn't get the glimpse of that guy eating a sandwich out of her head. *No one would do that in a physical meeting!*

On what felt like an impulse, she sent a quick message to Eric. "Sorry to bother you, I had a bit of a car crash of a meeting today, do you have time to talk tomorrow?" He replied almost instantly, "I'm pretty full but can spare half an hour first thing, does 8.30 work for you?" Kim did a quick calculation: if she dropped the kids at school 10 minutes earlier than normal, then she could be back in time. "Sure, thank you," she replied.

Kim dropped her bag and kicked off her shoes as she walked back in through her front door, glancing quickly at her watch. *8.23 am, perfect.* She made her way to the kitchen, grabbed a glass of water, and sat down for her meeting with Eric. *I seem to be having a lot of meetings with him lately!* They briefly caught up with how things were going and how they had been dealing with adjusting to life during the pandemic, after which they jumped into discussing Kim's meeting.

Kim related the meeting to him, explaining how she'd changed her presentation and introduced a story after the success she had with that earlier in the week.

"They just weren't giving me anything, even when I asked if anyone had any questions at the end of the presentation, all I got was a few 'nos' and some head shakes." Kim visibly slumped as she finished talking.

"It sounds like you didn't give them too many opportunities to give you much back," Eric said. "I really like what you've done with your presentation, and I think bringing in the story is great, but when we're meeting people virtually we've really got to think on another level about how we can keep bringing their attention back to us and what we're saying."

"Okay ..." Kim said, somewhat hesitantly. She understood what Eric was saying but she couldn't quite work out how to do that. *Everything feels different when it's virtual,* she wanted to say.

It was as though Eric read her mind. "Try to think of each meeting as more of a conversation than a sales pitch with a presentation," he explained. "Ask questions throughout your presentation to get people involved, even call people out by name if you think they're not paying attention, it's a great way to keep everyone on their toes!"

"So, you're saying I should break up my presentation even more, with these extra questions in between? What if the meeting takes a complete sideways turn?" Kim asked.

"Be selective about the questions you ask and how long the answers can be," Eric replied. "I'll send you some suggestions of how to do that so you can have a read, and we can have another talk about this next week if you want. Sorry that I don't have a bit more time today."

Kim nodded. "Thank you, I appreciate this."

Eric cracked a broad smile. "And Kim, don't feel bad, this happens to all of us. I had a guy fall asleep in one of my virtual meetings once. We learn from this and we move on, right?"

"Right," Kim said, feeling much more confident. She couldn't help but laugh. *At least none of my clients have fallen asleep on me!*

Why is it important to engage your customers virtually?

Engagement and trust are often the biggest barriers to having great virtual interactions. It is important to remember that it takes two people to have a meeting, and therefore you should create a dialogue. If you are delivering a monologue, you will not be engaging the other participants.

Engagement is one of the most difficult things to get right in a virtual setting. You can probably recall some of the fun facts of how prominent disengagement is during virtual meetings that we have touched upon in Chapter 2:

The Virtual Meetings Enemy #1:

DISENGAGEMENT

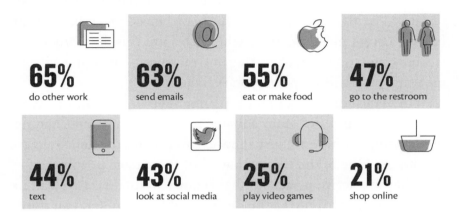

65% do other work	**63%** send emails	**55%** eat or make food	**47%** go to the restroom
44% text	**43%** look at social media	**25%** play video games	**21%** shop online

Survey by West Unified Communications Services in 2014 on 500 Americans

What this demonstrates is that you are much more likely to be disengaged than you are to be fully engaged for the entirety of a virtual meeting. People often do not dedicate their full attention to a virtual meeting, particularly if they do not even have their camera on.

If you look at the above statistics, you can see just how difficult it is to ensure that your participants are engaged. If we look at that data from your position as a salesperson, imagine how difficult it will be for you to succeed at making a sale if you are unable to get your participants to fully devote their attention to the virtual meeting and the content that you are sharing. To realise the full potential of virtual selling, it is key to ensure that your customers and prospects are engaged in your virtual interaction.

Why is engagement so difficult in a virtual setting?

Although the prevalence of virtual meetings has been accelerated by the Covid-19 pandemic, they are not completely new. As we discussed at the beginning of the book, most of us have been having virtual meetings for a while. Despite this, in many cases we have not quite cracked the nut of having engaging virtual meetings that will keep everyone's focus.

In a sales context, your meeting might be aimed at influencing others, making a decision, solving problems, or strengthening relationships. These are just a few examples, but the list could go on and on. One of the things that all of these have in common is that they are active processes that require participants to lean in and actively contribute to the desired outcome. When you think about it, this is a precondition to having an effective meeting in any setting, because the whole notion of a meeting is that you have two or more parties contributing to it.

Whether your meeting is virtual or physical, you need participants' voluntary engagement for it to be effective.

Accountability is key

A key challenge in virtual meetings, as identified by the Harvard Business Review,[1] is that in most virtual meetings participants have little to no accountability for their engagement. This is one reason why it is so difficult to have an engaging virtual meeting.

"Let's face it, most virtual meetings have always sucked because there's often little to zero accountability for engagement."
– Harvard Business Review 2020

Look back at the barriers that we explored in Chapter 2. One classic example is not having your camera turned on. If this is the case people cannot even see you, which means you could be doing anything else, especially if your microphone is also muted. In this instance, you might technically be in the meeting, but you are not voluntarily and practically engaging in the meeting. This underscores the necessity of overcoming the barriers we discussed earlier in the book.

Engagement by design

By their nature, virtual sales meetings are less likely to engage your audience, which is why it is important to design for engagement.

Often there is a significant disconnect between how we think we behave and what we actually do. For instance, 53% of sales reps believe that they tailor their content and the form of their meetings well to a virtual environment.[2] However, when asked what tools they used to secure engagement in a virtual setting, only 12% said they used interactive tools that create engagement in the virtual world.[3]

The disconnect between **perception** and **behaviour** in virtual meetings

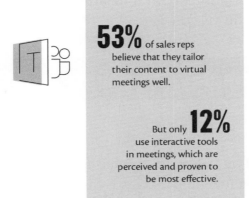

53% of sales reps believe that they tailor their content to virtual meetings well.

But only **12%** use interactive tools in meetings, which are perceived and proven to be most effective.

Now we are going to take you through some of the different types of engagements that you can include in your virtual meetings, as well as providing some tips and tricks for how you can make sure your virtual meetings are as engaging as possible for everyone involved.

Building energy for effective openers

Openers aim to get the meeting off to a good start, and this is half the battle when it comes to engagement in virtual meetings. If you are able to open your meeting with good energy, ensure that everybody feels engaged and involved, build trust, and make sure everybody has the opportunity to contribute, then you are setting yourself up for a successful meeting from the beginning.

This is why we recommend that you invite people for a five-minute coffee chat before the meeting officially starts. As we discussed in Chapter 2, this is a way to accelerate trust building. Rather than jumping straight into the agenda, you could do a quick roundtable or, if there are many participants, invite everyone to share something about themselves and introduce themselves using the chat function.

The important thing is to understand that overcoming the barriers of disengagement and a lack of trust require additional effort, and therefore it is important to plan some time into your agenda to create an effective opener.

Examples of openers

If it is a new customer ...

Introduce yourself by stating your name and where you are located in the chat function. This is a simple yet effective option if you have multiple meeting participants and it is a meeting with a new customer, or if there are some participants who you have not met before.

If it is an existing customer ...

In this case you may not need an introduction round, but you can use icebreaker questions instead to create that engagement. It might be following up on what you discussed last time, or if you know something personal about this customer, you could ask how their family is or how their holiday was. If you do not have that personal information, you could start by discussing something that is going on in their country, for example. This is about kick-starting a conversation.

Staging for engagement

As a facilitator, you want your participants to think, "I don't want to disconnect or disengage from this call." There are several ways in which you can create this feeling—some are technical and some are more human.

Simply how you present yourself at the beginning of the meeting is important. If you greet everyone with a big smile and say something like, "Morning guys, this is going to be great," in a really enthusiastic tone, you are showing them that you are engaged in the meeting, which will help them to engage in return. If, by contrast, you greet them in a monotone with a phrase like, "Morning, let's just get started," you are turning them off before you have even begun.

We talked about pre-engagement in Chapter 4, but this is a really important element to consider. Before the meeting, you could also ask some of your participants to take a more active role. This means they will come into your meeting with something to contribute, and they will not just be passive receivers.

An example of a pre-engagement task

If it is the first time you will be meeting with a particular company, you could ask one or two participants to put together just a four-minute talk to share highlights from the company and its most important priorities.

This will not only make them more engaged before the meeting, but it will mean that they come into that meeting with more energy and engagement too, because they know they will participate and contribute.

We mentioned tone of voice, but movement is also important when you are creating an engaging virtual meeting. You do not need to jump around, but you might lean in to share certain information or change your position during the meeting. This movement will simply help keep people's attention and focus and keep them engaged.

Having your camera on is therefore essential. We have mentioned this multiple times throughout the book, but that is because it is so important for reducing the barriers (physical, social, cultural, and technological) you experience in virtual meetings, and it is so simple. It is not only your camera that should be on; ask your participants to turn theirs on, too.

The point to remember with virtual meetings is that everyone is a passive participant unless you make them active by encouraging them to give you feedback and engage. Activating people in your meeting is essential for their engagement.

Open-ended versus closed questions

When you are facilitating a virtual sales meeting, it is important to understand the difference between open-ended and closed questions, as well as when it is appropriate to use each.

Our definition of a closed question is very simple: this is a question that can be answered with "Yes" or "No." An open-ended question is one that invites more elaborate discussion. You can use both types of questions as check-ins, which we will talk about in more detail shortly.

Phrasing **open** or **closed questions** allows you to control the length and depth of the micro-involvement

CLOSED QUESTIONS

Questions that can be answered with a "YES" or "NO", or a simple phrase

OPEN QUESTIONS

Questions that deliberately seek longer, more elaborate and in-depth answers

The benefit of closed questions in a virtual context is that, if you only need to break up your monologue but you do not have the time in the agenda for an elaborate question and response, a yes/no question will do the trick and catch the attention of anyone who might have been distracted.

Open-ended questions are designed to get the customer talking and to share valuable information that you can use later in the sales process. In essence, these types of questions are conversation starters to help you develop a deeper understanding.

CLOSED QUESTIONS

allow for time-efficient customer engagement and are well suited to confirm understanding and agreement

	useful for ...
• Fact-based	• Easy, not too revealing opening questions / icebreakers
• Easy to answer	
• Quick to answer	• Short engagements to grab attention / boost energy
• The Questioner retains control of the conversation	• Testing / confirming understanding
• Any question can be turned into a closed question by adding "isn't it?", "true?", "correct?" etc. in the end	• Breaking a long monologue
	• Closure confirmation

TOP TIP   You can set up a desired frame of mind in your participants by using successive questions with obvious yes / no answers.

---

example

OPENER   What is your name? / Have you been doing well?

CHECK-IN   Does this resonate with you? / How many product launches do you tend to do per season?

RECAP   You indicated that we will prioritise action X – is this true?

CLOSER   Do you agree with the next steps we have aligned on?

Mante's perspective

The practical importance of check-ins

While we were in the process of writing this book, I was in a meeting which presented the perfect example of why it is so important to use closed questions to test or confirm the understanding of the participants.

During a sales meeting, a colleague was delivering a sales presentation. The view was jumping around and it was difficult to know which slide she was on. I could tell that my view was not following the presenter's view and I was wondering whether this was the same for the customer.

Around 20 minutes into the presentation, the customer interrupted and asked which slide we were on, because what they could see was not matching what my colleague was talking about. For me this was the perfect example of why checking in with your participants to confirm they understand or that they are following your presentation is so important.

In a sales context, closed questions are also incredibly useful when you are explaining a value proposition. Once you have finished, use a closed question to confirm understanding: Does this resonate? Do you have any questions? Both of those require a yes/no answer and will help you confirm understanding before you continue. If your customer does have questions, this gives you the opportunity to go back, and you can follow up with an open-ended question.

OPEN QUESTIONS

are great conversation starters that allow you to get a deeper understanding of the customer

- Respondents are prompted to think and reflect

- Respondents will provide their opinions and feelings

- Usually begin with **what, why, how, describe etc.**

useful for ...

- Deep-diving on an interesting point shared by the customer

- Engaging passive participants

- Helping customers to realise the extent of their problem / the viability of your solution

TOP TIP Follow a closed question with an open-ended question to develop a conversation between your participants.

---

example

OPENER How have you / your business been affected by this trend?

CHECK-IN How do the market trends just presented resonate with you? / Tell me about the project you are currently running that you are most excited about?

RECAP Last time you told me that X, where are you with this initiative now?

CLOSER What are your key take-aways from today's meeting?

The virtual parking lot

One concern that you may have in using open-ended questions is that they can give control of the conversation to the respondent. In some instances, this can lead to the dialogue going off course, or it may simply be that what they are sharing is not constructive or adding value to the meeting.

In this case, we recommend using a technique called the virtual parking lot. You begin by saying, "Sorry to interrupt, that's a very good point," or "That's a good reflection," and then you explain that you will park it for the time being and address it either after the meeting, at a later stage in the meeting, or that you will reach out personally to that person so you can discuss it further.

This allows you to keep control of the agenda, without dismissing someone's contribution or offending them.

Although it is possible for someone to steer the direction of the meeting once you start using open-ended questions, there are other methods, in addition to the virtual parking lot, that you can use to keep the discussion on track.

For example, you can politely interrupt the person who is speaking and ask for another participant to share their perspective on what they have said. This can also be a useful tool if you have a few participants who are being rather quiet, as it is a way of encouraging them to contribute to the discussion.

Strategic importance of check-ins

Check-ins are a simple way of getting your participants to focus on what you are saying and keep them alert. They can have several uses in a virtual meeting, including to capture the attention of your participants, to check whether they have any questions or reflections, and to start a dialogue to break up your monologue. Fundamentally, they are a point at which you go from only being focused on your speech to something that actively involves the participants.

They are one of the most important micro-engagements you can use. However, when you engage your participants in a virtual meeting, it needs to be purposeful. This is not about asking nonsensical questions just to make sure that you are not the only one speaking, because people will notice and likely perceive it to be a waste of time.

The key to check-ins is to make sure that they add value to the conversation. This is essential to using check-ins strategically during your sales meetings. It is also important to prepare your check-in questions in advance of your meeting. This is because if you are well prepared before your meeting, with a few good questions that you can ask, you will feel more confident and comfortable during the meeting itself.

You can strategically use closed and open-ended questions throughout your meeting to navigate the length and depth of the engagements within your virtual meeting.

When you are introducing a check-in, especially after you have been speaking for a while, consider addressing your question to a specific participant using their name. This will not only show a personal touch but will also make people accountable for their engagement. For instance, if you ask someone a question and they are online shopping rather than paying full attention, chances are that they will stop online shopping and focus more on the meeting.

You can also use technology to help you with your check-ins. This means you can include these micro-involvements without having to break up your presentation too much. Simply asking everyone to put a thumbs up in the chat if they have understood what you have said so far or to indicate they can still hear you is often enough.

Close your PowerPoint for the check-in

Sometimes it is good to take your PowerPoint away, and this is particularly the case with your check-ins. Close your presentation and get everybody on screen, tell them they should all have their cameras on and that you are all going to discuss the slides they have just seen for 10 minutes. This is a really nice way to use your camera within a meeting to remove some of the physical, social, and cultural barriers that we have talked about.

You also have to remember that your PowerPoint can act as a barrier between you and your participants, so closing it while you have this dialogue is a good way to bring you closer to the other people in your meeting and help keep people engaged and alert.

Your virtual meeting challenge

We talk a lot about using PowerPoint, but consider whether your meeting needs a PowerPoint presentation. Ask yourself whether you would have a PowerPoint presentation if you were meeting in person. If not, try to host your virtual meeting without Power-Point, or at the very least reduce it to just two or three slides that underpin your key messages. This will allow you to increase the personal connection that you would have in a face-to-face meeting, and increase trust and engagement.

The power of recaps

Recaps are used to ensure understanding and alignment during a meeting before progressing to the next agenda point. Recapping is very important in virtual meetings due to the difficulty for participants to stay fully focused and engaged for long periods of time, as we have seen in the statistics of disengagements at the beginning of this chapter. So, what do you do if you find your participants visibly disengaged?

If you find yourself in a situation where your participants are not following your storyline anymore, recaps can help you get them engaged again. By placing recaps of the content covered strategically across your presentation and meeting, you will ensure that any participant that has lost focus and attention during the course of the meeting has the opportunity to jump back into following your agenda. Through strategically recapping, you will be able to turn passive participants into active contributors.

Best practice rules for engagement in virtual meetings

The following are a few very simple best practice rules to help encourage engagement in your virtual meetings.

Check in every five minutes

This will ensure that you are not just delivering a monologue. Micro-involvements are a great way to check the temperature of engagement in your meeting.

Presentations should be a maximum of 10 minutes long

This does not mean that you can only present a topic for 10 minutes. What we mean is that you should ensure you are not talking solidly for longer than 10 minutes during your presentation. Use the check-ins to help break it up, and design your presentation to include engagements every 10 minutes. Normally, our attention span is 20 minutes, but in a virtual environment it is even shorter.

Make your virtual meetings a maximum of 90 minutes long

This is not to say that you absolutely cannot go over 90 minutes in a virtual meeting, but be aware that the longer your meeting runs for, the more difficult it is to maintain people's attention, trust, and engagement.

Preparation is especially important for longer virtual meetings, and as we mentioned in Chapter 4, you need to be aware that the longer your meeting is, the more taxing it will be for you as the host. Consider including more breaks in a virtual meeting than you would in a face-to-face meeting. This will give your participants a chance to listen to that voicemail or answer the text message that they might otherwise be tempted to respond to during the meeting.

Important **numbers to remember** when facilitating virtual meetings

Check in every
5 minutes

Presentations maximum
10 minutes

90 minutes
in total

Mante's perspective

The Importance of micro-engagements

I was once delivering a workshop on engagement in virtual meetings and I asked the participants why micro-involvements are important. One person responded that they're important because they had once had someone fall asleep in one of their virtual meetings. The only reason he noticed this had happened was that the person who fell asleep didn't leave at the end of the meeting!

A suggested timeline for a virtual meeting

Suggested virtual meeting timeline

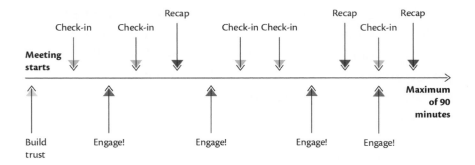

Leveraging closers

From an engagement perspective, closers are important in virtual meetings for several reasons. Firstly, because some people may not have felt able or been willing to contribute. Secondly, leveraging closers at the end of your meeting can help prevent misalignment and misunderstandings that are much more common in a virtual setting than in the physical world, due to the physical, social, cultural, and technological barriers that we outlined in Chapter 2.

This is especially the case if your participants do not have their cameras on, and you cannot see their reactions to what has been discussed. If you have delivered a monologue, without checking in as you go, the chances of misunderstandings and misalignment in a virtual environment are further amplified. This means you could leave the meeting feeling that you are aligned, when in fact the opposite is true.

We will talk about closers in more depth in Chapter 7, but from an engagement perspective it is important to use closers in the final stages of your meetings to clear up misunderstandings, clarify any questions, and ensure that everyone is aligned before you leave the meeting.

IDEA IN *brief*

- To realise the full potential of virtual selling, it is key to ensure that your customers and prospects are engaged in your virtual interaction.

- Engagement is difficult to achieve virtually, because there is little personal accountability to proactively contribute to the meeting outcome in a virtual setting.

- This means that virtual meetings need to be designed to support and nudge engagement – which can be effectively facilitated through openers, check-ins, recaps and closers.

- We explore concrete and hands-on tips and tricks for effective virtual engagement throughout the chapter.

Build trust and drive impact

Engaging your participants is important for building trust. In the next chapter, we are going to look at how you can effectively build trust in the virtual world and provide you with specific tips and tricks to help you improve the impact of your virtual interactions when executing virtual meetings.

Chapter 7:

EXECUTING THE VIRTUAL SALES MEETING

Do you trust me?

Kim was tapping her pad with her pen, clock-watching and knowing she didn't have long until her sales meeting started. *What if this goes completely off track? How can I keep the meeting running smoothly if I introduce all these discussions? What if I don't get through my presentation because we're talking too much?*

Kim took a deep breath and had a sip of water. You can do this, she told herself. A quick glance at her workstation showed her that everything she needed was there. She was about to make another coffee when she stopped herself. Caffeine is not what you need when you're already full of energy!

She sighed, sat down, and opened her presentation, glancing at her notes and the list of questions she had written down as prompts to ask at various points during the meeting.

Here we go, she thought, as she opened the meeting, positioned herself in front of her camera, and made some final adjustments to her appearance. The first of the five people joining the meeting arrived just a few minutes later.

"Morning Kim," Jenny said. "I know I'm a bit early, but I hate feeling like I'm the last one to join these meetings!"

Kim smiled. "I know, it's nice to feel as though you've just got a few minutes to gather your thoughts and make sure everything's working, isn't it?" As the others gradually joined the meeting, Kim introduced herself and made a quick note about each person in the meeting. Once everyone was present and the chatter had died down, Kim said, "Shall we get started?"

After just 10 minutes, Kim paused her presentation to ask her first question. She turned off her screen share. "I know we're only just getting started, but are there any areas where you can see how our product could help in your operations?" *Should I direct that question at someone if no one answers?* Just as Kim was worried that her meeting was stalling already, Jenny jumped in with an answer. Within a minute, she was having an animated conversation with Tim, who, according to Kim's notes, was part of the procurement team.

Kim relaxed, but she was aware she still had a lot to cover. She waited for a natural break in the conversation and then jumped in. "Thank you for your input, that's really useful and it's great to hear that you can see the potential this can unlock. Let's dive a bit deeper into the product and continue this discussion shortly."

All eyes were on Kim as she reopened her PowerPoint and continued. As the meeting progressed, Kim relaxed more and more. She could feel everyone starting to get excited about the possibilities, and each time they broke for a brief conversation she learned more about what they needed as a business.

In the final 10 minutes of the meeting, they put together an action plan setting out their next steps, and Kim booked a second meeting for the following Tuesday. As she ended the call, Kim glanced at her notepad. It was full of useful bits of information that would help her move this sale forward. She stretched and smiled.

An hour later, she was putting the finishing touches to her follow-up email outlining everything that was discussed and what actions were agreed on by both her and the client. She hit send and sat back in her chair. Within a few moments, she saw a response from Jenny pop up in her inbox.

Dear Kim,
Thank you so much for your time today. We had a quick debrief call after our meeting and we all agreed that we feel as though you understand what we're looking for and that we can really trust you to help us move the business forward. We're looking forward to what comes next and speaking with you again next week.
Kind regards,
Jenny

Kim broke into a huge smile and tapped out a reply. *Now I think it's time for coffee!*

One of the key focuses when executing a virtual sales meeting is building trust. In this chapter, we are going to look in detail at the importance of building trust in virtual customer engagement, as well as sharing some tips and tricks to help you build trust with your customers when executing your own virtual meetings.

What is trust?

Trust is fundamentally all about feeling safe. Within relationships, it means believing in someone else's strength and integrity to the extent that you are able to put yourself on the line at some risk to yourself. Trust is essential for an effective team because it provides a sense of safety.

To put this more into the context of virtual sales, it is the concept that your customers believe you are taking care of their best interests.

Why is building trust so important?

Before we look at trust in a virtual environment, it is important to consider why building trust is important in any sales meeting, regardless of the medium you hold it in. As we mentioned in Chapter 2, human collaboration is rooted in trust.

From a sales perspective, we know that people do not buy from people they do not trust. If your customer does not trust you, they are not going to feel safe putting their business in your hands. That means if you do not build trust you will struggle to convince your customer to meet with you in the first place, and it will also be more of a challenge to get them to authentically and honestly share their pain points and provide the data you need.

This, in turn, will make it more difficult for you to design a value proposition that resonates with the customer, creating a significant barrier to success. Of the four barriers that we explored in Chapter 2, it is primarily the physical and social barriers that result in a lack of trust.

When you meet physically, trust is created through several channels. It is not only created through what you say and how you say it but also through your body language. Mark Bowden, a body language expert, even explains that if people cannot see your hands, then subconsciously they will not trust you. This is rooted deep in our evolution, because we are hard-wired to think that if someone is hiding their hands, they may have a concealed weapon.

As soon as you put people in a virtual environment, a lot of the channels we use to build trust are taken away. Therefore, we keep talking about how important it is to have your camera switched on, as this will allow people to see at least some of your body language. You can also alleviate the barrier relating to your hands by elevating them so that they can be seen on the camera.

This lack of trust can manifest even in established teams, let alone with clients with whom you are having your first virtual interactions. Research[1] has found that the perceived level of trust within established teams is likely to drop by 83% when the team interacts virtually rather than in the same physical space.

Without trust, meetings become less effective, people disengage more quickly and are typically more hesitant about sharing their ideas or opinions. Although we have been using virtual meetings for a while, for many of us they still feel new. When something is new to you, it is likely to activate your threat response, but this threat response can be fought by building trust.

How to start building trust in your virtual meetings

How to build **trust** in your virtual meeting

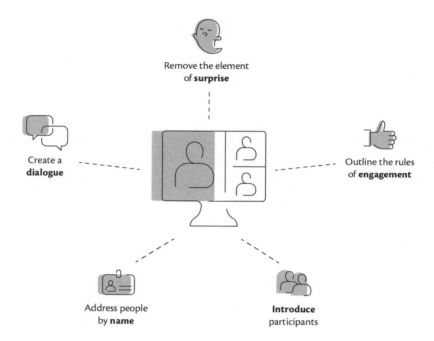

Remove the element of surprise

One of the best things you can do to build trust is take the element of surprise out of the equation. Evolutionarily speaking, surprise was bad because it meant danger. In the same way that many of us do not like change, we also do not like surprises, which in turn leads to resistance.

To start building trust, you first have to acknowledge that many of your customers will still be resistors to this virtual way of meeting and selling. In fact, as many as one in five of your customers is likely to still be a resistor. One of the ways to overcome that resistance is to take the element of surprise out of the meeting.

This means that the very first step toward building trust comes before you hold your meeting. This comes back to all of the preparation we discussed in Chapter 4. That means you have to make sure your customer knows what they are walking into in terms of what you will be discussing, as well as understanding what you are trying to achieve in the meeting and having a clear view of the agenda.

Eliminating the surprise also refers to the technology that you will be using and how you will be conducting the meeting. Tell them in advance that they will be expected to have their camera on, because this will help them prepare and allow them to find a suitable location for your meeting. If you take them by surprise by asking them to turn on their camera, you are likely to activate their threat response and in doing so diminish trust.

Outline the rules of engagement

Outlining the rules of engagement is an important part of building trust between you and your participants. This is when you tell people upfront what they can expect, but it also serves the purpose of keeping your participants engaged.

This is especially important for overcoming the cultural barriers we discussed in Chapter 2. For example, if you have participants from high power-distance or hierarchy-driven societies and you have not told them upfront that it is okay for them to interrupt you with questions as you go along, they might just stay quiet. That does not mean they do not find your content interesting or that they are disengaged by default; it is simply that due to their cultural background they will not interrupt you out of respect.

There are two sides to this, but very briefly setting out rules for engagement and interaction at the start of a virtual meeting is important both to let the participants know that they will be expected to engage and be active in the session rather than passively listening and that it is okay for them to ask questions and interrupt if there is something they do not understand.

Introductions to lay the foundations for trust

At the beginning of your meeting, it is also important to provide a short, formal introduction for every participant in the meeting. We gave you some suggestions of how you can do this quickly and efficiently in Chapter 2 when we discussed overcoming barriers within virtual meetings.

> **Top tip:** Introductions do not have to be verbal. Make use of the technology that you have in the virtual world. You could ask everyone to introduce themselves in the chat function. Or you could share an interactive map and ask people to put a pin in it to show their location.

This is one example of where the virtual setting can improve the process. We are sure you have all been in physical meetings where it seems that people talk about themselves for a long time during this introduction round. You can avoid this completely in the virtual.

It is also important to remember that often virtual meetings tend to be shorter and include fewer people than do face-to-face meetings, particularly if you would travel long distances for a physical meeting with a client. This means virtual meetings often feel different to physical ones, particularly at the beginning.

As the facilitator, it is good to acknowledge that this might be new for some people and for you to take control of the introductions and take responsibility for starting the meeting in this way. Start by saying, "I know virtual might be new to some people, but let's just have a short round-the-table introduction like we would if we were all together. It's just nice to start by hearing everyone talk." Taking responsibility in this way and demonstrating that you know it is a different environment will make you come across as genuine, and this will help you build trust with the participants.

Address people by name

As the facilitator, it is important to address people by name in a virtual setting, because this helps you to build trust. This is also a useful tip because it means you can be clear who you are directing a question at—thereby avoiding the dreaded silence at the other end when you ask an undirected question in a virtual meeting and people do not know who should answer first.

In a physical environment, you would look at the person you were asking, but this is not possible when you are separated by a screen, which is why it is necessary that you are specific when you address your participants.

When you address people by name, you are making it very clear who you are talking to. This will allow you to engage your participants, get the desired input, and lead your meeting effectively.

Top tip: Have a list of all the participants' names at hand if you think you will struggle to remember everyone's names.

This will also enable you to note down specific things that participants say that you can come back to later in the meeting. This will give your participants the impression that you are fully present, acknowledge their input, and make them feel important.

Create a dialogue

It can be very easy to slip into a monologue, especially in a virtual setting, but to build trust we need to have dialogue. You want your customer to come out of the meeting and feel as though they have been heard and as though they have been given the opportunity to share their perspective.

Look at the response Kim got when she took the time to listen to her customer. We all want to feel as though we have been heard, and to create that in your virtual sales meetings you need to give people the opportunity to speak. One way of encouraging that is *active listening*.

Active listening[2] is when you fully immerse into your customer's communication—from the words they say, to their tone of voice and body language—and respond back by confirming your understanding of the key points they share. This confirmation response can start with:

"What I am hearing is …"
"I understand that your key point is …"
"Is it correct that your key pains are …"

This will prompt your customer to add more reflections to your point of interest and help you build rapport, engagement and trust. A great tip we live by is *"Be interested instead of interesting."* Most salespeople are trained to speak instead of listen and hence can end up overfocused on elaborating on product or service attributes to make the sale instead of putting the customer center stage. To truly understand customer needs, which is a prerequisite for making a sale, listening is key.

Some tips on how you can practice active listening in the virtual world include:

- Focus fully on what your customer is saying instead of formulating your response in your head.
- Dare to close down PowerPoint (if you are using it) into gallery view so you can mimic eye contact as much as possible and thereby enhance the feeling that you are listening to your customer.
- Ensure your body language reflects that you are listening; beyond eye contact, ensure you nod, smile, use emoticons in the virtual medium (for example, a thumbs-up or smile emoticon reaction in Zoom).

- Paraphrase the speaker's key ideas to reflect that you are listening and confirm your own understanding.
- Ask open-ended questions to encourage more in-depth responses.

Top tip: Active listening is a useful skill to develop because it not only ensures that your customer will feel heard but also gives you a way of buying time when you are answering questions and will help you ensure that you have understood what has been said or asked of you.

How to close a virtual meeting

As we mentioned in Chapter 6, closure of your virtual meeting is important because there is a higher likelihood of misunderstandings or things going unsaid in a virtual environment than in a physical one. Closure is your opportunity to check for four elements: completion, alignment, next steps, and value.

- **Completion:** Check whether anyone has anything else to say or anything they would still like to express.
- **Alignment:** Check that everyone is okay with where you have ended up in the conversation.
- **Next steps:** Check that everyone is clear about what actions come next, who will take those actions, and when they should be completed by.
- **Value:** Check to find out what value everyone is taking away from this conversation.

When you reach the end of your conversation, make sure you cover each of these four elements of closure. This is vital for eliminating misunderstandings both on your side and the side of your customer.

CLOSURE ⇨ Wrap up each conversation deliberately using the four elements of closure:

1 Check for COMPLETION

Does anyone have anything else to say or ask that has not yet been expressed?

Fill in here

2 Check for ALIGNMENT

Is everyone okay with where we ended up in this conversation?

Fill in here

3 Check for NEXT STEPS

Are we clear about who will take actions and when those actions will be finished?

Fill in here

4 Check for VALUE

What value are you taking away from this conversation?

Fill in here

Securing an effective follow-up

Following up after a meeting is something that you would do in the physical world as well as the virtual, but you can follow up slightly differently in the virtual world and even include part of this process in the meeting itself.

Plan to spend time at the end of the meeting to wrap it up and agree on the next steps. Build this into your agenda to ensure you have time to start the follow-up before you all leave the virtual meeting room.

Generally speaking, the follow-up from any meeting is done in the form of email. There are several reasons for having a written follow-up rather than simply relying on a verbal one.

Firstly, it ensures that there is a common understanding of your discussions so far. Secondly, it will help your customer to perceive you as an organised and thorough professional. Thirdly, you can use the content as background information further on in the sales process. Finally, you avoid misunderstandings later in the process when you ask your client to respond to your follow-up email.

While all of these benefits come from sending a follow-up email, we believe there is an additional benefit to agreeing on the next steps during the virtual meeting, and simply reiterating those in the follow-up.

Ending your meeting by agreeing the next steps will allow you to leverage the positive energy you have created, as well as using the momentum you generate with your effective closure to agree to the next touchpoint.

On a purely practical note as a salesperson running virtual meetings, it is much easier to compare calendars and agree on when you will next touch base when you are all still in the virtual meeting room, rather than sending calendar invites back and forth. Ultimately, planning some of the follow-up process into the agenda for the actual meeting will make you more effective.

Using the follow-up to create engagement

When you invite your customer to co-create with you, you are promoting their engagement ahead of your next virtual meeting. Use your follow-up to invite them to be an active participant in the meeting and use their insights to help you plan more effective sales meetings.

Top tip: Invite your customer to give their take on what should be the key agenda points and objectives for the next meeting. This will help you from both a sales point of view and in terms of building engagement. Understanding what resonated and where you should focus your attention will help you prepare a more effective next meeting. This insight from your customer will also allow you to build an effective agenda. Taking this approach front-loads the engagement, because it enables you to position this meeting not as "your meeting" but as a meeting that you are having together with your customer. This means they know they are taking an active role in the meeting; they also have ownership and feel responsibility to have a good interaction.

This tip is valuable to any salesperson and it will help lift some of the weight off your shoulders in your role as the facilitator. This is also vital for driving engagement because, all of a sudden, this meeting is not about you, it is about creating value for your customer. That in turn helps to drive up win rates and can help increase virtual customer engagement throughout the rest of the sales process.

It is what we describe as the virtual IKEA effect; the concept being that you love your IKEA furniture because you have assembled it yourself. In the context of a virtual meeting, this means you are more likely to fall in love with what you are doing in these virtual meetings if you feel like you have actually contributed to them.

Our top three ways of creating engagement and ownership

1. Create a separate point on the agenda to create alignment for the next meeting within your first meeting.
2. Create alignment for the next meeting by following up via email.
3. If there are many stakeholders, arrange a brief, 15-minute call with each ahead of your meeting to position yourself for commercial impact and get closer to the stakeholders to ensure you are all aligned.

Our top three technical tips for building trust

1. Always have your camera on—and ask participants to do the same.
2. Let people know they can always use the chat to ask questions or use the "raise your hand" function if they want to chip in with a question or comment.
3. Elevate the PC so the camera is at the same level as your eyes.

Our top three personal tips for building trust

1. Address people by name.
2. Include something personal in the background of your video.
3. Communicate your meeting purpose, agenda, and expectations from participants in advance to remove the element of surprise.

Our top three body language tips for building trust

1. Put a smiley face drawn on a Post-It note under your camera to encourage you to look at it and smile while you are talking, as this will mimic looking into someone's eyes and smiling face.
2. Make sure that people can see your hands in your video.
3. Lean in toward the camera.

IDEA IN *brief*

- Building trust is a key element in order to secure desired meeting outcomes when executing virtual sales meetings – but is difficult to achieve and nurture in a virtual setting.

- To build trust in your virtual meetings, it is important to remove the element of surprise, by letting your meeting participants know what will be expected of them in advance.

- Outlining the rules of virtual engagement, introducing the meeting participants, addressing people by name and creating a dialogue also help to build trust in a virtual meeting room.

- Effective closure of a virtual meeting allows you to eliminate the risk of misunderstandings later in the sales process.

- An effective follow-up after your virtual meeting allows to accelerate decision making and frontload customer engagement for the next virtual meeting.

A time of transformation

By now, you will hopefully understand how effective virtual sales meetings can be when they are prepared and executed effectively. In the final chapter, we will explore how your role as a salesperson will need to evolve to accommodate virtual selling alongside face-to-face meetings, as well as diving into the executive perspective on the transformation to a virtual sales model.

Chapter 8:

LEADING THE TRANSFORMATION FROM PHYSICAL TO VIRTUAL SALES

Finding the balance

As Kim stirred with the sun light shining through the crack in the curtains, she stretched out in bed and reached for her phone. She idly scrolled through her calendar to check what she had in for the day. Just two meetings this morning, a block of time to prepare for her performance review with her line manager, then one more meeting before she had to pick the kids up from school.

She smiled at the thought of meeting her son and daughter at the school gates. *Collecting them on Friday afternoons has certainly been less stressful since I've been working from home*, Kim thought. She stretched once more before carefully climbing out of the bed and navigating the step.

I'm getting a bonus this month, this step is going! She smiled at the thought, remembering her painful tumble and collision with the wall as lockdown was beginning.

In the kitchen, Kim turned on her laptop while making coffee. *I should probably create a more permanent office space*, she thought to herself, as she surveyed not only her laptop, but her headset and notepad that were spreading across the kitchen counter. As she opened her emails, she saw three from clients who she'd met with this week.

All were positive. One in particular made her smile as she sipped her first cup of coffee of the day.

Dear Kim,

Thank you so much for your time on Wednesday. We found your presentation very engaging and informative, and we very much appreciated having the opportunity to speak to Eric about our specific technical requirements in detail. Yours was by far the most professional and useful presentation we saw this week. Having reported to our board, we would like to meet again to discuss moving forward with the deal.

Have a lovely weekend,

James

And to think how much I hated virtual meetings just a few months ago! Kim sent a reply to James and made sure to mark the email in her inbox. That's one to use for my performance review!

One of the things her manager had asked her to do was to compile a list of all the meetings she'd attended in the past six months. This kind of admin task was not Kim's favourite, but she knew it was necessary. As she worked her way through her calendar, she realised that she was now averaging 15 meetings a week. That can't be right, normally five a week would be a stretch .... She paused and double-checked her figures. No, she was right—15 a week. *Wow, maybe there are more benefits to virtual meetings than I thought!*

Kim stared at the figures on the pad in front of her. *Not only am I seeing more clients, and making more sales, but I'm not stressing about being late to collect the kids from school and I've even found time to virtually catch up with friends in the evenings in the past few months....* Her thoughts were interrupted by her alarm warning her that her final meeting of the day was in 15 minutes. She set her notes for her performance review to one side, opened her slide deck, and popped to the bathroom before logging into Zoom. This meeting would finish at 2.30 pm, giving her plenty of time to finish her admin before she had to get to school for the kids.

As she walked home with her daughter chattering excitedly about her day, and her son slaying imaginary adversaries ahead of them, Kim couldn't help but smile. She loved these moments with her kids. The school pickup was a far cry from how it used to be, with Kim arriving often 10 minutes late, frazzled and stressed, to find her son and daughter waiting patiently with their teacher and among the last to be collected. Hurried apologies and a mad dash home followed, with Kim usually collapsing on the sofa and the kids switching on the TV.

Now they enjoyed their walk back to the house, and Kim would make them all a snack when they got in. For half an hour, it was just the three of them, before the kids disappeared to their rooms to do their homework or play on their own. As they walked through the front door, Kim gave a contented sigh.

The kids didn't know it yet, but she had a day out at the zoo planned for them all tomorrow. *I love that I don't wake up every Saturday feeling exhausted after a week of travelling.* As Kim headed to the kitchen, her phone pinged. It was a message from her manager thanking her for the figures and confirming her performance review on Monday. *Now that's one meeting that I am looking forward to!*

How is your sales role evolving?

Before the Covid pandemic, the typical salesperson would have one meeting a day, which would involve a lot of preparation as well as travel time to get to the client. The effort and time involved in setting up this meeting would usually mean that you would only see clients when necessary. For existing clients that might only be once every six months.

How has this changed with the introduction of more virtual sales meetings? We are sure that you have noticed that you are having more meetings in a week. Instead of one a day you might have up to five. Consider how this is helping you to build stronger relationships with your customers. If your focus is on finding new customers, this will allow you to reach out to a much greater number of new prospects each week.

If you are working with existing customers, it means you can have more regular, shorter, and more valuable touchpoints with them to help maintain your relationships and solve problems as and when they arise. Because these meetings are shorter and more focused, you will have to do less preparation for them than you would if you were intending to deliver one long presentation.

However, this is far from the only way in which sales is evolving. As a salesperson in a virtual world, you have become a connector of people. By having more meetings in your sales process, you can help your customer connect the different decision makers. You can also add value by introducing experts from your business to work closely with experts in your customer's business.

Instead of selling one to one, you are now using the virtual environment to sell many to many.

As a salesperson, you are the one who will need to work out who you need to be speaking to on the customer side and how you can best connect them with the right people on your side. Would it help if your supply chain manager met with your customer's supply chain manager? Or can your customer's quality department have a conversation with someone in your quality department?

By facilitating these small interactions, you are not only adding value to the customer, and thereby increasing the chances of making a successful sale, but you are also making the sales process easier for yourself and giving yourself time to reach out to even more customers.

As we saw with Kim in our story, this can give you more time to spend with the people you love or doing activities you enjoy outside of work. Travelling less will be beneficial for your health, as we explained at the beginning of the book, as well as for your stress levels and, of course, for the environment.

However, we do not believe that the future is 100% virtual. A hybrid strategy is what we advocate for, and it seems to be what an increasing number of businesses are exploring.

What has happened since the Covid pandemic?

The Covid pandemic forced many organisations and salespeople alike to explore the opportunities available in the virtual world.

In the Chinese language, the word "crisis" is made up of two symbols, one of which symbolises danger and the other of which symbolises opportunity. What the pandemic has demonstrated is that, for many of us, we need the danger to be present—in this case, the threat of not being able to do business—in order to see the opportunities. For many of us working in sales roles, the pandemic has vastly accelerated our leap into the virtual world.

In a webinar that we hosted in September 2020, a quick poll of the participants (there were around 100 people present) showed that the vast majority (90%) plan to pursue a hybrid model in the future, with a small percentage (5%) going fully virtual and even fewer (just 2%) who plan to return to working the way they did before the pandemic.

What is interesting is that, even before the pandemic, there was a strong rationale for switching to a greater number of virtual interactions. Arguments such as being able to double the face time you have with your clients, as well as developing a more sustainable and robust sales model still applied before Covid came along.

There is plenty of evidence to show that contacting your customers more frequently and having shorter interactions with them each time drives customer satisfaction. However, without this necessity, many of us were stuck in our ways, and it is only now that we have been forced to take a different approach that we are truly appreciating the benefits it offers.

Christian's perspective

A personal change story

Prior to the Covid pandemic, I would always host my meetings face-to-face when possible. I would travel to visit customers for just a half-hour or hour-long meeting. If I'm being completely honest, I would have described myself as a virtual dinosaur, someone who resisted virtual interactions at every opportunity.

Then the pandemic happened, and I, like many others, no longer had any choice over whether I conducted my meetings in person or virtually. What I've discovered in the months since the pandemic began (which at the time of writing is six months) is that there are many benefits to hosting more meetings virtually.

For example, in one week I had 19 virtual interactions with people from all over the world. One day I had a meeting with 20 people from China in the morning and another meeting with 19 people from the United States in the afternoon. In between those two meetings, I hosted a webinar where I was speaking to close to 100 people from all over Northern Europe. That is just one brief illustration of how the pandemic has changed how I work.

On a personal note, I've learned that I can have both breakfast and dinner with my family, as well as touching base with people in China, the United States, Australia, and elsewhere in Europe. This period has also made me realise how easy it is to get a lot of people together in one virtual space to make a decision.

I hosted one sales meeting that included five country managers, where they were able to make a decision in that meeting. In the past, reaching that same decision would have required me to host many meetings and travel a considerable distance. For me, this really highlights the opportunities we have in a virtual setting.

Why stick with virtual in the future?

Our research found that 60% of the customer meetings we used to have physically can be converted to a virtual setting. We also discovered that the same percentage of customers are open to meeting virtually. Our survey revealed that 70% of organisations are likely to run virtual customer meetings in the future. This supports what many of us were already aware of: that many businesses have made the transition to virtual.

What is particularly interesting, however, is that another study[1] found 75% of B2B buyers believe that virtual sales interactions are more effective than physical ones.

Clearly, if your customers prefer virtual sales meetings, this is a compelling reason to continue operating virtually even as we emerge from the pandemic, and virtual once again becomes a choice rather than a necessity.

However, other research[2] also found that just 27% of B2B companies consider their new virtual sales model to be more effective in terms of customer acquisition and customer care, compared to their previous way of working. There is a disconnect here between the experiences of our customers and our experiences as salespeople.

This is one of the motivations for writing this book. There is growing evidence that the virtual sales model can be just as effective as selling face to face when it is done right, but there is still resistance to operating in this way, as well as a lack of consistent and thorough training to enable salespeople to excel in the virtual space.

Although there are barriers to overcome, both within ourselves, within our organisations, and among our customers, there has never been a better time to embrace virtual selling. The social distancing rules as a result of the Covid-19 pandemic mean that not only are we unable to meet many of our customers and prospects in-person, but that our commercial frontline has more time available as a result.

This is an opportunity to accelerate the introduction of current and new digital tools at your organisation, which will enable you to come out of the other side of the pandemic with more mature digital capabilities, alongside a sales model that is more sustainable and costs your business less.

Our research into virtual customer engagement found that there is a clear preference for a hybrid engagement model among the companies we surveyed. As we already mentioned, 70% of respondents to our survey stated that they are likely to run virtual customer meetings in the future, with 60% revealing that they will conduct a higher proportion of their customer and sales meetings online than they did before the Covid pandemic.

We also found that 74% of the companies we surveyed can see the value in blending the virtual with the physical and believe that they can create an even better experience for their customers by mixing virtual and physical touchpoints. Even if you return to some face-to-face meetings, you are likely to be conducting a greater number of interactions virtually than you were before the pandemic.

The business benefits of embracing virtual

Once you have accepted that virtual is here to stay, the next step is to rethink the commercial operating model to build a sales model that is more fit for the future and that allows you to reap the benefits that come from the virtual customer engagement model.

What we have seen in the early months of the Covid-19 pandemic and what we have found from our own research is that customers are generally willing to transition to virtual meetings: our survey found that six in 10 customers responded positively to requests for virtual meetings.

Efficiency

One of the key benefits that we have identified from moving toward a more virtual customer engagement model is increased efficiency, specifically in freeing up more time for sales activities and engaging in a greater number of and higher quality customer engagement points.

The respondents to our survey self-reported that they could free up approximately one-fifth of their monthly working time by moving from physical customer touchpoints to primarily virtual customer touchpoints.

Given the challenges businesses in every sector are facing as a result of Covid-19, any steps toward greater efficiency in the sales process while also improving customer engagement are to be welcomed.

Why are virtual sales meetings more efficient than their physical counterparts? Firstly, you are eliminating the need to travel, which saves a considerable amount of not only time but also money.

Secondly, as our survey shows, virtual meetings tend to be shorter and more to the point. Sixty-three percent of the respondents to our survey said that this was the case for their virtual meetings. Reducing the length of the meetings themselves and removing the need to travel are why operating a more virtual sales model provides so many efficiency gains.

Again, you have to frame this in the context of how you can best spend this additional time. Your sales team could devote more time to sales activities or use this additional time to increase the frequency of their interactions with their existing customers.

As we discussed in Chapter 2, there are the four main barriers (physical, social, cultural, and technological) that need to be overcome in order to have successful virtual meetings. Of course, not every meeting is best held in a virtual setting and, as we outlined in Chapter 3, a hybrid sales model is likely to become the most popular in the future. However, if you are able to mitigate and eliminate the main barriers to good virtual meetings, 60% can successfully be translated into the virtual setting.

Effectiveness

When you adapt your meeting format and style to suit the virtual world, you can improve your win rate. Over half (57%) of the executives we surveyed agreed that, by adjusting the content and form of sales presentations and supporting materials for the virtual environment, the win rate can be improved.

As we explained in Chapter 5, this means you are altering your PowerPoint presentation to suit the virtual medium, rather than using the slides and presentation you would have used in a face-to-face setting.

This additional attention and focus on the form and content of your virtual sales presentations to identify the specific value proposition and messaging for each client are what can help increase the impact you have in these virtual meetings and therefore improve your win rate.

Another key benefit from both a business and personal perspective of hosting at least some meetings virtually is that doing so shortens the sales cycle. If you eliminate the need to meet customers in person, you are more likely to be able to gain access to key stakeholders at key points in the sales cycle.

Our research found that 40% of executives believe it is easier to get key stakeholders to attend a virtual sales meeting than a physical one. This, in turn, can reduce the length of the sales cycle.

Another key business benefit to moving toward a greater volume of virtual customer engagements is the ability to leverage your business's global talent. Eliminating the need for people to physically travel to sales meetings opens the door to subject matter experts joining at key points during the sales process.

The findings of our research supported this, with 37% of respondents revealing that it is easier to include subject matter experts in meetings when they are held virtually. Giving customers access to your experts is important for driving up the success rate of your virtual sales meetings.

The benefits of embracing virtual

Increased efficiency
– free-up time for more and higher quality engagements

 20%
Less travelling provides more time (and saves costs)

 63%
Virtual meetings are shorter and more to the point

 60%
Physical meetings that can be converted to virtual

Increased effectiveness
– increase win rate and shorten sales cycle

 57%
Rethinking value messages and adapting presentations to a virtual format improves win rates

 40%
Easier access to more stakeholders shortens the sales cycle

 37%
Access to subject matter experts is likely to be better in the virtual environment

The lasting impact of Covid

Although the initial shock of the Covid-19 pandemic has dissipated, its impact will continue to be felt for months if not years to come. Travel restrictions are likely to be in place for some time to come.

Local lockdowns will be a consideration. Travelling to certain countries will be challenging if your salespeople are required to quarantine on their return. Some of your customers may introduce policies that prevent external visitors from going to their offices due to the health risks.

As we write this book, we are all settling into this "new normal," but it is important to accept that there will be various measures in place for some time that will prevent us from simply returning to how we used to operate. The hybrid scenario we outlined in Chapter 3, and earlier in this chapter, is likely to become our "new normal."

We believe there are two main ways of adopting this hybrid model. They are interlinked, and one does not exclude the other. The first is what we call virtualisation with impact. This essentially means looking at what we used to do and finding a virtual way of replicating it. The second is reinventing the sales model, which means looking at what we used to do and finding new ways of approaching these activities that are better suited to a virtual environment.

Combining the two will give you the best of both worlds. You will have what you used to do, but virtually enabled, and you will be able to adopt new ways of interacting with customers, as well as new business models, because you have seen that interacting virtually with customers is feasible for your business.

Two approaches to virtualise the sales model

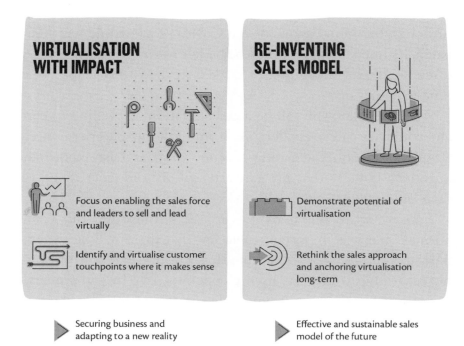

VIRTUALISATION WITH IMPACT	**RE-INVENTING SALES MODEL**
Focus on enabling the sales force and leaders to sell and lead virtually	Demonstrate potential of virtualisation
Identify and virtualise customer touchpoints where it makes sense	Rethink the sales approach and anchoring virtualisation long-term
▶ Securing business and adapting to a new reality	▶ Effective and sustainable sales model of the future

How to find opportunities to transition from physical to virtual interactions

Virtualisation with impact

This is fundamentally tooling up what we normally do. It does not require a change to our market focus, incentive systems, or any other elements of the traditional commercial operating model. It is simply a way of enabling and training the commercial frontline to do what they were already doing, but virtually.

This will involve training your salespeople in basic virtual meeting capabilities, not only from a technical perspective but also in terms of how to engage with an audience and build trust: everything that we have discussed in previous chapters.

Why upskill your team?

The correlation between meeting quality and how comfortable salespeople are with running virtual meetings highlights the need to invest in capability building to help sales teams navigate the change.

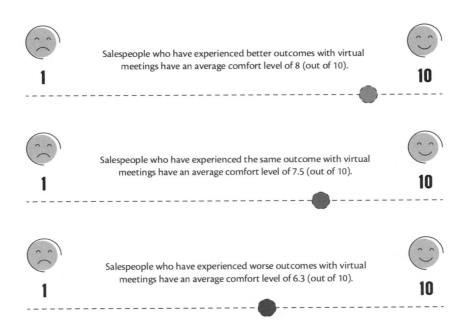

Upskilling your salespeople is essential to enable them to succeed in virtual sales meetings and customer interactions. As you will discover a little later in this chapter, there is a strong correlation between meeting quality, the positive outcome of virtual customer meetings, and the comfort level of the salesperson driving that customer meeting.

Broadly speaking, salespeople fall into three categories when it comes to the adoption of virtual selling: virtual embracers, late adopters, and virtual resistors. Of these three groups, you will need to do the most work with the virtual resistors to get them onboard.

Virtual resistors are typically the least comfortable operating in a virtual environment and, as a result, report experiencing worse outcomes with virtual meetings. Our research found that the people who report worse outcomes from virtual meetings than physical ones have a comfort rating of 6.3 out of 10. Compare this to those who report better outcomes from virtual meetings than physical ones, who have a comfort rating of 8.0 out of 10 in the virtual environment.

Upskilling everyone, but especially these virtual resistors, can therefore improve their comfort levels in virtual meetings and lead to better outcomes from those interactions. The good news is that virtual meeting capabilities are trainable, and you can strengthen your commercial teams by supporting and investing in training to help them navigate this transition toward greater virtual customer engagement.

How to adopt virtualisation with impact

Adopting virtualisation with impact is possible for many lead generation activities. For example, you could use social selling as a means of lead generation. You could explore running virtual seminars as a way of delivering insights to a greater number of customers. Or you could host virtual trade fairs.

Within customer acquisition, this could involve virtual product demonstrations and company tours and offering presentations. For customer development, you might introduce virtual maintenance, annual reviews, or new product presentations.

With this approach, you are looking at all the ways you used to work and identifying the virtual equivalent. Over time, this will allow you to present two options to your frontline sales team. One is how they can have that interaction virtually, and the other is how to have it in-person. It is important to understand that although they might both be the same kind of interaction, such as a product demonstration, the way in which you run them will look different depending on whether they are hosted virtually or face to face.

This is where the training that you offer is so important, because it will support your sales team's capability to support what you are doing. When you take this approach at your business, you are gradually converting interactions to the virtual space, where it makes sense to do so, while continuing to have physical interactions where these deliver a greater advantage.

Virtual interactions are not only useful in terms of how you deal with customers. From a leadership perspective, they can present tremendous opportunities in terms of leading a team. By introducing more frequent but shorter interactions with your team, you can better steer behaviours and priorities. There is no longer a need to gather everyone together in one physical space for a monthly meeting, because you can have weekly catch-ups that save time and are likely to allow you to lead more effectively.

Key takeaway: If you simply look at how you used to do things, you will see plenty of opportunities to virtualise those interactions. This can lead to significant benefits, including a higher level of meeting activity, lower travel costs, a healthier workforce, and lower CO_2 emissions. To virtualise with impact, skills, tools, and new habits must be designed and trained at each level.

Reinventing the sales model

Reinventing the sales model takes this concept to the next level. We have all learned something new during the Covid pandemic. This is where creativity comes in. You are not just replicating, you are reinventing.

Do you remember the case study we shared in Chapter 3, about improving service with virtual interactions? This is where a customer requested fewer meetings in a year, but for some of these to be held virtually with the logistics expert, rather than having a higher frequency of meetings in-person with the local account manager. This came about after the customer had a virtual meeting with a logistics expert due to the Covid situation and recognised the value that this expert could deliver to their business.

The reason we are reminding you of this story now is that this was a learning for the company in question. Through this interaction they realised that if they put their experts in front of their customers all over the world, they could create more value than their local salespeople might be capable of.

This is about looking for new ways of working virtually, in addition to face to face, that enable you to create an even better customer experience. When you open it, you will realise that this is a Pandora's Box of opportunities.

The following are just four examples of learnings that we have seen among our customers that show how the virtual world can be used to add value and improve your existing process.

1. **Experts engaging virtually:** Experts used to be a scarce resource, but as soon as their time is not taken up with travelling, they are able to meet more and a wider range of customers.

   Imagine the amount of value you can add if, instead of your expert only being able to have one meeting per week with two days of travelling either side, they can participate in six, seven, or even eight meetings in a day? This is an example of reinventing your engagement model to introduce a new way of sharing your expertise with your customers.

2. **Virtual qualification:** This is an opportunity to prequalify sales opportunities. On average, close to 50% of the opportunities in a company's customer relationship management system will come to nothing. You may spend a lot of time and effort working on them and trying to sell to them but end up with no sale at the end of it. This is largely because leads are not prequalified. You have to ask why you are sending an

expensive salesperson to visit someone without any prequalification. Establishing a prequalification team who can work virtually has multiple benefits.

Firstly, it will save you pursuing leads that are unlikely to result in sales. Secondly, it allows you to identify key priorities for each potential customer. If your salesperson then goes to a meeting with this prospective customer, just imagine how well prepared they will be and, therefore, how much more likely they are to make a sale.

Of course, some companies already prequalified their leads, but when you do this at the scale that virtual customer engagement enables, you can have a significant impact on the effectiveness and efficiency of your sales process.

3. **A greater number of small customer acquisitions:** The cost to sell to customers using a virtual model is significantly lower than for physical meetings. For many companies, this has opened up a number of new potential customers that they would not normally serve due to the cost of the sale.

   Another opportunity to emerge, therefore, is to have a dedicated small customer acquisition team that is purely virtual. They can address all the customers that your business would not normally send a salesperson to. This same team could also act as a customer care team, taking care of all the smaller accounts and giving those customers the same feeling of presence that larger customers get through physical meetings.

4. **Bite-size inspiration meetings:** Instead of starting out with an hour-long new sales meeting, consider inviting your potential prospects to a 20-minute inspiration meeting where you get straight to the point and inspire them about your product or service. You could even get another customer to dial in and share this experience.

These are just a few examples to illustrate how many different or new models emerge when you look to the virtual world for opportunities to create new interactions. Considering these ideas, as well as combining them with other virtual and physical interactions can help you reach more new customers or improve the levels of satisfaction among your existing customers.

Key takeaway: This approach is about inventing new ways to reach new customers and to interact with existing customers. Although your customers may not initially be used to your new approach, they may come to prefer it. To realise the benefits of virtual sales in the long term, organisations need to rethink their sales model.

Two approaches to virtualise the sales model

Reaping the benefits of virtual in a hybrid model

If we accept that the hybrid model is the future of sales, then we need to adopt both the approaches (virtualisation with impact and reinventing the sales model) outlined above. Virtualising what we used to do is a good first step, but to really reap the benefits of virtual in a hybrid model, we also need to reinvent our interactions.

Our recommended path to success in this new hybrid world is to begin by designing the hybrid engagement model. That means identifying your key new touchpoints and thinking about which existing meetings you could convert to virtual. This step is about setting your ambitions in terms of what you want your future model to look like.

Once you have done this, it is time to rethink and decide what the new virtual touchpoints will look like. When you start inventing new touchpoints, you have the opportunity to add significant value to your customers, but you also have to accept that making this choice is likely to mean you need to change some of the existing structures at your company.

Zoom in on the most important customer touchpoints and then define your new model where you combine the virtual and physical to provide your customers with the best experience.

The next step is to rethink both your content and your messaging for virtual settings. Long PowerPoint presentations do not work in a virtual setting. For virtual interactions, your messaging needs to be incredibly clear, and we recommend including fewer points to better suit this new environment. Although rethinking your content is a huge task, remember that doing so means you are more likely to increase your win rate.

Developing the digital tools, virtual tools, and playbooks to support new conversations and strengthen capabilities at your organisation is also essential. In our experience, a lot of the resistance to these new ways of working comes from a lack of confidence among salespeople.

Most salespeople have never been trained in using primarily virtual interactions with customers. As a result, many are not confident in their ability to engage with customers using virtual tools. In our research, decoding body language, building trust, technical issues, and engaging customers virtually were cited as the greatest barriers to succeeding in virtual sales meetings.

Key barriers to virtual sales meeting success

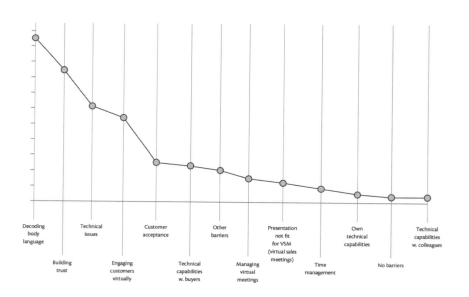

Key barriers can be overcome with training and capability building to succeed with virtual sales meetings.

When you recognise that you do not currently have the skills to master virtual interactions, you also acknowledge that a change in your behaviour is required. However, knowing that change is necessary can activate your fight response, particularly if you are a virtual resistor.

We know that trust is key to building salespeople's confidence and we also know that improving salespeople's levels of comfort in virtual meetings helps them to build trust with their customers and this in turn gives them more confidence.

Therefore, if you can increase your team's confidence, you can more than likely reduce the level of resistance you experience to adopting this new model, as well as improve the outcomes they experience in their virtual sales meetings. Finally, your commercial leadership conversations should support this new model.

Are you ready for the move to virtual?

Increasing your confidence and comfort levels in the virtual world is key to having successful virtual sales meetings. Our research found that, broadly speaking, people fall into one of three categories when it comes to their acceptance of virtual customer engagement:

- Virtual embracers
- Late adopters
- Virtual resistors

In our survey, 46% of respondents were classified as virtual embracers. This means they intend to pursue a virtual engagement model in the future and have increased their number of sales meetings by going virtual.

Thirty-four percent of respondents are what we call late adopters. They also intend to pursue a virtual engagement model in the future, but unlike the virtual embracers they have not yet increased their number of sales meetings by going virtual.

Finally, 20% of respondents were classified as virtual resistors. They have no intention of pursuing a virtual engagement model in the future and have not yet engaged with virtual modes of interaction.

These findings show that there is still a clear split between the organisations that are open to change and want to leverage the benefits associated with a more virtual customer engagement model and those that are focusing on getting back to the "old reality."

The key for any business that wants to adopt a more virtual way of interacting with customers, but that is encountering resistance from some of its sales team, is to look for ways to move people along the change curve. This is possible, and in many ways it comes down to helping people feel confident in their abilities in a virtual environment.

Let's explore the main characteristics of the people who fall into each of these three categories.

Virtual embracers

The people in this category have the ability to create impactful and high-quality virtual meetings. As a result of that experience, they will not revert back to their old ways of working—66% of virtual embracers claim that the quality of virtual meetings can either be the same or better than physical meetings.

Eighty-six percent of virtual embracers believe that we can provide a better customer experience by adopting a hybrid customer engagement model that blends virtual and physical touchpoints. Only one in four of the people in this group believe that customers will revert to the old way of working when the restrictions imposed due to the pandemic ease.

Late adopters

The people in this group plan to pursue a hybrid model of customer interactions in the future, but they still need to develop their virtual meeting capabilities to help them better adapt to the virtual customer engagement model.

Essentially this means that as they develop their capabilities and skill set, they will feel more confident and comfortable in the virtual medium and therefore move along the change curve toward becoming a virtual embracer.

Sixty-nine percent of these late adopters believe that combining virtual and physical touch points will result in a better customer experience, and seven in 10 of them will conduct a higher proportion of their sales meetings in a virtual setting in the future.

However, just over half of this group believe that the outcomes of virtual meetings are relatively worse than physical meetings. Again, this suggests that they could improve the outcomes of their virtual meetings by developing their own skills and toolbox to use in virtual customer interactions.

Virtual resistors

The people in this category typically have a low level of comfort in virtual settings, rating their average comfort level when running virtual sales meetings at 5.4 out of 10. As a result, seven in 10 of them intend to return to their old ways of working when the restrictions end—56% of this group also believe that transitioning to a virtual sales model is not supported by customers.

However, their low comfort level in a virtual environment is one of the key drivers for this, and it is therefore essential that, as an organisation that is moving toward a more virtual way of working, you help these people to develop their skills and knowledge in this area to improve their confidence and comfort levels.

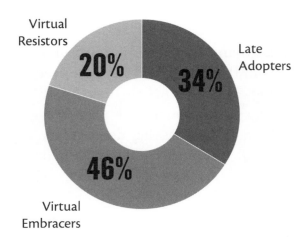

○ 46% Virtual Embracers
Respondents who will pursue the
virtual engagement model in the future.

○ 34% Late Adopters
Respondents who will pursue the virtual
engagement model in the future.

○ 20% Virtual Resistors
Respondents who will not pursue the
virtual engagement model in the future.

As a business, if you want to transform toward a more virtual model of customer engagement, it is vital that you focus your efforts on helping your virtual resistors and late adopters to progress along the change curve.

Our research has found that confidence and competence are strongly correlated to virtual meeting outcomes. Salespeople who said they had experienced better outcomes with virtual meetings had an average comfort level of 8.0 out of 10.

Those who said they had experienced the same outcome with virtual meetings as with physical ones had an average comfort level of 7.5 out of 10. However, those who experienced worse outcomes in virtual meetings had an average comfort level of 6.3 out of 10.

With that in mind, it is clear to see why building the virtual skills and capabilities within your sales teams is so important for effecting change and moving toward a more hybrid way of working.

It is also important to give your virtual embracers a voice and to allow them to share some of their positive stories about virtual meetings to help others further behind them on the change curve to understand what is possible when virtual meetings are done well.

What we would like you to take from this research, and this book as a whole, is that it is possible to train people to become more competent and confident in delivering virtual meetings. This will drive success in virtual settings.

This capability is like a muscle that we can strengthen by investing in training and support to help commercial teams navigate the transition toward a greater level of virtual customer engagement.

The key area we focus on to kickstart this transformation is confidence and giving salespeople more confidence when interacting with customers online. Remember that many people operating in commercial roles have never been trained to deliver virtual meetings. This way of interacting is new to them, but by providing appropriate training and support you can encourage everyone in your sales team to embrace this virtual way of working.

How comfortable are you in virtual sales meetings?

Do you remember when we asked you how comfortable you are in virtual sales meetings at the start of this book? How would you answer that same question now?

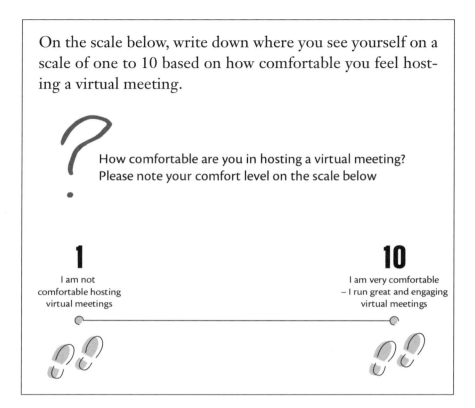

On the scale below, write down where you see yourself on a scale of one to 10 based on how comfortable you feel hosting a virtual meeting.

How comfortable are you in hosting a virtual meeting? Please note your comfort level on the scale below

1

I am not comfortable hosting virtual meetings

10

I am very comfortable – I run great and engaging virtual meetings

Maybe your answer is the same as when you started reading this book. We hope, however, that your confidence and comfort levels have improved because you now have some tools you can use to deliver more impactful virtual meetings with your customers.

Training for successful change

Your training for successful change should focus on three areas:

1. **Confidence:** Increasing the personal level of comfort in leading virtual interactions with customers.
2. **Competence:** Building the skills and capabilities needed to effectively engage customers in a virtual setting.
3. **Toolbox:** Supplying salespeople with hands-on tips and tricks that can be applied immediately.

Delivering training that focuses on these areas will help you and the rest of your sales team to facilitate high-quality virtual meetings that have high levels of engagement.

How to get started with your virtual operating model

Virtual operating model

Design the hybrid engagement model.

Rethink how you engage in your virtual touchpoints.

Develop digital tools to support conversations.

Rethink your content and messaging.

Strengthen virtual engagement capabilities.

Adjust commercial leadership conversations.

Case studies

To show you just how much impact adopting a hybrid sales model can have, we are sharing some of the case studies we have gathered in recent months with you here. We always love to hear about other organisations' experiences of transitioning to a more virtual sales model. If you have any stories you would like to share, and that you feel could be included in a second edition of this book, please send them to us at maku@implement.no or cmj@implement.dk.

Recognising the savings from lockdown

One business that we are working with has identified a significant upside to transitioning to a virtual sales model as a result of the lockdown during the Covid-19 pandemic.

During the four months of lockdown in 2020, this company saved an average of €1 million per month in travel costs alone. Given that the average salesperson at this organisation expects to convert around 40% of their physical meetings to virtual meetings in the future, the company has calculated that it can save around €4.8 million a year in travel costs by switching to a hybrid model of customer engagement.

Direct savings as a result of people travelling less is not the only benefit. There is also potential for revenue growth. Remember, salespeople travelling to fewer meetings frees up 20% of this organisation's time. When you look at that 20%, you can see how you can create a few more opportunities.

For instance, if this organisation can increase the number of sales opportunities it has by 10%, increase its win rate by just 10%, and reduce the length of the sales cycle by 5%, it can realise a 29% increase in sales revenue. That is without increasing the average deal size it gets from its customers.

This is just one illustration of how you can not only make direct cost savings by adopting a hybrid way of working, but also how this can translate into revenue growth at the same time.

Upskilling to adapt a new customer engagement model

One of our customer's sales models was heavily based on physical interaction. Their lead generation relied heavily on large trade shows and exhibitions, and the customer engagement model required a lot of physical collaboration in their lab and face-to-face meetings.

During Covid, they realised that they needed to reinvent their overall customer engagement model—from lead generation to sales follow-up activities. They realised that even when the pandemic was over, it would be highly unlikely they could leverage large-scale exhibitions to the same extent as before or that their customers would be open to meeting external partners in person.

They understood that their previous fully physical customer engagement model needed to go virtual. So, they decided to redirect their trade exhibition investments toward upskilling their commercial frontline with the skills and capabilities needed to effectively engage customers in a virtual setting.

Together, we decided to start with "low-hanging fruit"—upskill to ensure engaging and effective virtual customer meetings. But we also put up a long-term vision: to host a virtual "trade show," including virtual demo meetings of their latest innovations, in order to virtually generate a strong sales pipeline.

This not only gave the commercial organisation the needed skills and capabilities to effectively engage their customers online but also united the team around a common bigger purpose during a turbulent time.

IDEA IN *brief*

- There is growing evidence that virtual sales can be just as effective as selling face to face, and that virtual will remain an important part of the future sales model.

- The business benefits of embracing virtual customer interactions range from increased efficiency to increased effectiveness.

- We believe there are two ways of adopting the hybrid sales model: virtualisation with impact and reinventing the sales model.

- Virtualisation with impact refers to enabling and training the commercial frontline to succeed with your current sales model in a virtual setting.

- Reinventing the sales model refers to rethinking your sales approach to adapt an effective and sustainable sales model of the future, that reaps the full benefits of virtual interactions.

Conclusion

By now you will hopefully have a good understanding of the typical barriers to good virtual sales meetings and you will have plenty of tools to help you overcome those barriers, but there might be just one thing preventing you from doing a really great job in your virtual sales meetings: your fear of not being perfect.

Even if you are confident delivering presentations in face-to-face meetings, you may find you are overly critical of yourself when you bring this into the virtual world. In a virtual environment, you may well be out of your comfort zone, and as you are trying to grapple with this new normal, it can be easy to get caught up in feeling as though every meeting has to go perfectly and worrying that the people attending your meetings will be judging you for doing a bad job.

Christian's perspective

I was recently leaving the office when I met one of our customers, who had come in to be filmed for a training video we were producing. She was really dressed up, so I complimented her on her outfit. Then I asked her, "How did it go?" She replied, "I think it went well, but I really wonder what people will think when they see me on the video. I think I was a little bit stiff because of the circumstances."

I told her that she is probably the only person who's thinking about how other people will perceive her. I'm sure everyone who watches that video will relate to what she says, rather than analysing her performance.

Put aside perfection

It is very easy in a virtual environment to worry about what other people think of you. Our advice is to put aside that desire for perfection. If you can leave behind your concerns about what other people are going to think of you when you enter a virtual interaction, then you will do a much better job.

You might even feel as though you do not want to host a virtual meeting at all until you have perfected all the skills we have discussed, but you will learn and grow the more virtual interactions you have. No one expects you to perform perfectly in every meeting. In fact, we are willing to bet that often when small things go wrong in a virtual meeting the only person who will notice them is you.

Embrace the uncertainty and the things that do not go exactly to plan. Recognise that it is the little imperfections that make us human and that help others relate to us and build trust.

Accept that technology can fail, and instead of focusing on that as a problem, look for a solution that you can use. Use the interruptions, like your children appearing in the room, to your advantage to show your personality and build trust.

Mante's perspective

I was recently in a sales meeting with a client when the WiFi collapsed and we lost our connection. I was trying to work out whether it was a problem on her side or mine, because my WiFi appeared to still be working. I simply phoned her and she explained it was a problem on her end.

We continued the meeting on the phone, and I sent her a copy of my presentation so she could still see my slides. In the end, we lost about three minutes, but other than the WiFi issue, the meeting went as planned.

Remember you are speaking to people

Another common fear is one of public speaking. As a salesperson, you might be used to having one-to-one interactions and all of a sudden, in the virtual environment, you are attending meetings with more participants than you usually would.

Just because you are having these interactions virtually does not mean this inner fear of public speaking will go away. In some cases, it can even be amplified because you are unable to sense the energy among your participants in the same way that you would if you were all in a room together.

Our advice to overcome this fear is to be yourself. Be authentic and do not fall into the trap of believing that you have to dress or behave in a certain way to be perceived as professional in a virtual setting. You are having meetings with other people, and, although hosting meetings virtually might feel different, remember that you are still speaking to another person or people on the other side of the screen.

These are the final hurdles to overcome in your virtual interactions. Trust your skills, trust your knowledge, and trust yourself and you will notice the difference in the quality and outcomes of your virtual sales meetings.

Call to action

If you are an innovator or early adopter, you have probably been virtual for quite some time by now, and by reading this book, you might have found a few tips or tricks to improve your virtual interactions going forward. We hope you will continue your virtual sales journey and help the world change a little bit by increasing your reach and impact while minimising your CO_2 emissions (reduced travelling) and having more time for your friends, relatives, and hobbies.

If you are a late adopter or even a virtual resistor, you have probably not yet started or even acknowledged the benefits of virtual selling. We hope this book has helped prepare you for a more virtual future, and given you tools, tips, and tricks to start your personal virtual sales journey. The good news from our research is that the only thing that seems to separate virtual first movers from late adopters and virtual resistors is their level of confidence in conducting virtual meetings. And how do you build confidence? You build confidence from doing it, again and again, and learning to improve every time. So, our advice to you, if you are a late adopter or virtual resistor is: Just do it! By just doing it, you will learn something new every time and gradually improve and increase your virtual confidence. And following your first five to 10 virtual customer meetings, the likelihood is that you too will learn to love Virtual Selling.

Epilogue

It was late Friday afternoon, and Kim was subconsciously already in weekend mode when an incoming Teams call appeared on her screen. She was surprised to see it was Paul calling. *Did I forget a late meeting*? she thought to herself, while looking for the headset she had learned to love in the past couple of days. Kim picked up the call, while seamlessly connecting the headset and checking the calendar on her phone—there was no appointment scheduled this afternoon.

"Hi Paul," she said with confidence, "How can I help you?" Paul's face appeared on her screen as he turned on the camera. He had a smile on his face, which made Kim lower her shoulders just a little bit.

"Hi Kim," Paul replied, "How are you?"

"I'm good. Almost ready to start my weekend! How are you?"

"I'm good. I have looked forward to this call since yesterday afternoon where we had our final internal evaluation meeting," He paused....

The pause was just long enough for Kim to notice her heartbeat go up. "Really?" she replied, and without giving it a thought, she continued.... "Should I open a bottle of wine?" She smiled to the camera, and Paul smiled back.

"Well, the contract is yours, so if that calls for a glass of wine, I suggest you go get a nice bottle. I already have a glass of white wine here on my desk, so maybe we can make a virtual toast to celebrate?"

Paul's reply made Kim cheer so loud that she could see Paul laugh. "Just a second, I'll go get a glass of wine," she said.

On her way to the kitchen, Kim couldn't help dancing and cheering. She was so happy with the news that she totally forgot she was still wearing the headset. On the other end of the virtual line, Paul smiled and thought to himself, *I'm really looking forward to this collaboration. Every virtual interaction with Kim has its surprises, so imagine what it will be like to have her visit our office someday. In the end, showing her true self and being open to feedback and making adjustments along the way were what tipped the coin in her favour*, Paul concluded.

References

Bain & Company (2020). Virtual B2B Selling is here to stay, June 2020.

Caldarola, R. (2011). The Interaction of Three Dimensions of Trust, Relational Selling, Team Selling and B2B Sales Success in the European Market. *International Business & Economics Research Journal* 8. 10.19030/iber.v8i1.3084.

Captio.com. (2016). Blog post mentioning findings (27 July 2016). https://www.captio.com/blog/how-does-business-travel-affect-your-personal-life Original report: Captio, 1st Report into the Personal impact of Corporate Travel, https://cdn2.hubspot.net/hubfs/260057/Descarregables/EN/CAPTIO_Report_Captios_1st_Report_into_the_personal_impact_of_corporate_travel.pdf?utm_campaign=Corporate%20traveller%20-%20Business%20travel%20EN%20jul16&utm_medium=email&_hsmi=31645614&_hsenc=p2ANqtz-VNWCmWYwuK_39qBBBVwN7agE6blYIXuyA8e7gi3FjKs96HWREK0-hVMDuno1kmcSfJ5dceKku9oXSM-7ZkjcTERpLVw&utm_content=31645614&utm_source=hs_automation

Centre for Body Language: https://centerforbodylanguage.com/ // https://www.youtube.com/watch?v=FphvDnSUiys

Corporatevisions.com (2018). State of the Conversation Report, The Next Best Thing to Being There, Sept. 24, 2018.

CSO Insights (2018). 2018 Buyer Preferences Study.

Deloitte: HBR: Getting Virtual Teams Right (2014). The Art of Building Trust on Virtual Platforms, 2020.

Dewan, P. (2015). Words Versus Pictures: Leveraging the Research on Visual Communication. *Partnership: The Canadian Journal of Library and Information Practice and Research*, *10*(1). https://doi.org/10.21083/partnership.v10i1.3137

Harari, Y. N. (2015). *Sapiens: A Brief History of Humankind*. New York: Harper.

Harvard Business Review (2014). Getting Virtual Teams Right. Hbr.org.

Harvard Business Review (December 2015). https://hbr.org/2015/12/proof-that-positive-work-cultures-are-more-productive

Harvard Business Review (2017). https://hbr.org/2017/03/the-new-sales-imperative

Harvard Business Review (2020). How to Get People to Actually Participate in Virtual Meetings. Hbr.org.

Harvard Business Review (2020). The Art of Building Trust on Virtual Platforms. Hbr.org.

International Workplace Group (March 2019). https://www.iwgplc.com/MediaCentre/PressRelease/flexible-working-is-now-a-deal-breaker-in-the-war-for-talent

Lieberman, M. (2013). *Social: Why Our Brains Are Wired to Connect*. New York: Crown Publishers.

Lojeski, K. (2015). The Hidden Traps of Virtual Teams. Harvard Business Review.

Lufthansa Group, April 6 2020.

McKinsey B2B Decision-Maker Pulse Survey, 8 April 2020 (Article: The B2B digital inflection point: How sales have changed during Covid-19).

Medium (October 2019). https://medium.com/@cooleffect/how-to-reduce-the-environmental-impact-of-business-travel-1f66bfd1cc3

MIT: https://news.mit.edu/2014/in-the-blink-of-an-eye-0116 https://www.researchgate.net/publication/332380784_How_many_words_do_we_read_per_minute_A_review_and_meta-analysis_of_reading_rate http://misrc.umn.edu/workingpapers/fullpapers/1986/8611.pdf

Pauser, S., Wagner, U., Ebster, C. (2018). An Investigation of Salespeople's Nonverbal Behaviors and Their Effect on Charismatic Appearance and Favorable Consumer Responses. *Journal of Personal Selling & Sales Management* 38:3, 344–369, DOI:10.1080/08853134.2018.1480383

Pease, A., Pease, B. (2006). *The Definitive Book of Body Language*. New York: Bantam Books.

Perreault, C., Mathew, S. (2012). Dating the Origin of Language Using Phonemic Diversity. *PLoS ONE*. 7 (4): e35289. Bibcode:2012PLoSO...735289P. doi:10.1371/journal.pone.0035289. PMC 3338724. PMID 22558135.

PhiX (February 2020). https://phixtechnologies.com/financial-uncertainties-business-travel-expenses/

Raconteur (May 2018). https://www.raconteur.net/business-innovation/reducing-corporate-carbon-footprint

ResearchGate (December 2008). https://www.researchgate.net/publication/227640576_Organisational_Effectiveness_and_Customer_Satisfaction

Rosenblum, L. D. (2010). *See What I'm Saying: The Extraordinary Powers of Our Five Senses*. New York: W.W. Norton & Company.

Rundle, A. G., Revenson, T. A., Friedman, M. (2018). Business Travel and Behavioural and Mental Health. *Journal of Occupational and Environmental Medicine* 60(7), 612–616. Available from: https://journals.lww.com/joem/pages/articleviewer.aspx?year=2018&issue=07000&article=00006&type=Abstract&sessionEnd=true

Statista (2020). https://www.statista.com/statistics/674328/average-international-business-trip-costs-faced-by-us-travelers/ and https://www.statista.com/statistics/675026/average-domestic-business-trip-cost-us/

Stephens, G. J., Silbert, L. J., Hasson, U. (2010). Speaker–Listener Neural Coupling Underlies Successful Communication. *Proceedings of the National Academy of Sciences*, Aug. 2010, 107 (32) 14425–14430; DOI: 10.1073/pnas.1008662107

Survey by West Unified Communication Services, 2014.

Survey (on 500 Americans) by West Unified Communications Services, 2014.

Travelport (2018). https://raconteur.uberflip.com/i/1151288-future-of-business-travel-2019/5?m4=

Willis, J., Todorov, A. (2006). First Impressions: Making Up Your Mind After 100 ms Exposure to a Face (PDF). *Psychological Science* 17(7): 592–598. doi:10.1111/j.1467-9280.2006.01750.x. PMID 16866745. Archived from the original (PDF) on 15 July 2014. Retrieved 17 May 2014. https://www.rochester.edu/pr/Review/V74N4/0402_brainscience.html https://citeseerx.ist.psu.edu/viewdoc/download?doi=10.1.1.720.6969&rep=rep1&type=pdf

Words Versus Pictures: Leveraging the Research on Visual Communication, Pauline Dewan, Wilfrid Laurier University file:///C:/Users/olbj/Downloads/3137-Article%20Text-18708-4-10-20150624.pdf

Notes

Introduction

1. State of the Conversation Report, The Next Best Thing to Being There, Sept. 24, 2018.
2. Ibid.

Chapter 1

1. Lufthansa Group, April 6, 2020.
2. Blog post mentioning findings (27 July 2016): https://www.captio.com/blog/how-does-business-travel-affect-your-personal-life
   Original report: Captio, 1st Report into the Personal Impact of Corporate Travel, https://cdn2.hubspot.net/hubfs/260057/Descarregables/EN/CAPTIO_Report_Captios_1st_Report_into_the_personal_impact_of_corporate_travel.pdf?utm_campaign=Corporate%20traveller%20-%20Business%20travel%20EN%20jul16&utm_medium=email&_hsmi=31645614&_hsenc=p2ANqtz--VNWCmWYwuK_39qBBBVwN7agE6blYIXuyA8e7gi3FjKs96HWREK0-hVMDuno1kmcSfJ5dceKku9oXSM-7ZkjcTERpLVw&utm_content=31645614&utm_source=hs_automation
3. Travelport 2018: https://raconteur.uberflip.com/i/1151288-future-of-business-travel-2019/5?m4=
4. Assuming 200 working days per year, 10% value-creation during travel time, 80% value-creation during customer time, 40% value-creation during admin/other time.
5. Harvard Business Review, 2017: https://hbr.org/2017/03/the-new-sales-imperative

6. Rundle, A. G., Revenson, T. A., Friedman, M. (2018). Business Travel and Behavioural and Mental Health. *Journal of Occupational and Environmental Medicine* 60 (7), 612–616. Available from: https://journals.lww.com/joem/pages/articleviewer.aspx?year=2018&issue=07000&article=00006&type=Abstract&sessionEnd=true

7. ResearchGate, December 2008: https://www.researchgate.net/publication/227640576_Organisational_Effectiveness_and_Customer_Satisfaction

8. Statista, 2020: https://www.statista.com/statistics/674328/average-international-business-trip-costs-faced-by-us-travelers/ and https://www.statista.com/statistics/675026/average-domestic-business-trip-cost-us/

9. PhiX, February 2020: https://phixtechnologies.com/financial-uncertainties-business-travel-expenses/

10. Harvard Business Review, December 2015: https://hbr.org/2015/12/proof-that-positive-work-cultures-are-more-productive

11. International Workplace Group, March 2019: https://www.iwgplc.com/MediaCentre/PressRelease/flexible-working-is-now-a-deal-breaker-in-the-war-for-talent

12. Raconteur, May 2018: https://www.raconteur.net/business-innovation/reducing-corporate-carbon-footprint

13. Medium, October 2019: https://medium.com/@cooleffect/how-to-reduce-the-environmental-impact-of-business-travel-1f66bfd1cc3

Chapter 2

1. Corporatevisions.com, State of the Conversation Report, The Next Best Thing to Being There, Sept., 24, 2018.

2. Deloitte: HBR: Getting Virtual Teams Right, 2014; The Art of Building Trust on Virtual Platforms, 2020.

3. Harvard Business Review, March 2020: https://hbr.org/2020/03/how-to-get-people-to-actually-participate-in-virtual-meetings

4. Survey (on 500 Americans) by West Unified Communications Services, 2014.

5. Perreault, C., Mathew, S. (2012). Dating the Origin of Language Using Phonemic Diversity. *PLoS ONE* 7(4): e35289. Bibcode:2012PLoSO...735289P.

6. Pease, A., Pease, B. (2006). *The Definitive Book of Body Language*. New York: Bantam Books.

7. Willis, J., Todorov, A. (2006). First Impressions: Making up Your Mind After 100 ms Exposure to a Face (PDF). *Psychological Science* 17(7): 592–598. doi:10.1111/j.1467-9280.2006.01750.x. PMID 16866745. Archived from the original (PDF) on 15 July 2014. Retrieved 17 May 2014.

8. Pauser, S., Wagner, U., Ebster, C. (2018). An Investigation of Salespeople's Nonverbal Behaviors and Their Effect on Charismatic Appearance

and Favorable Consumer Responses. *Journal of Personal Selling & Sales Management* 38:3, 344-369, DOI:10.1080/08853134.2018.1480383

9. Centre for Body Language: https://centerforbodylanguage.com/ // https://www.youtube.com/watch?v=FphvDnSUiys
10. Lieberman, M. (2013). *Social: Why Our Brains Are Wired to Connect.* New York: Crown Publishers.
11. Caldarola, R. (2011). The Interaction of Three Dimensions of Trust, Relational Selling, Team Selling and B2B Sales Success in the European Market. *International Business & Economics Research Journal* 8. 10.19030/iber.v8i1.3084.
12. Lojeski, K. (2015). The Hidden Traps of Virtual Teams. Harvard Business Review.

Chapter 3

1. Harvard Business Review (March 2017): https://hbr.org/2017/03/the-new-sales-imperative
2. CSO Insights, 2018 Buyer Preferences Study

Chapter 5

1. Survey by West Unified Communication Services, 2014.
2. Max-Planck-Gesellschaft, April 15 2008, Decision-making May Be Surprisingly Unconscious Activity, ScienceDaily: https://www.sciencedaily.com/releases/2008/04/080414145705.htm
3. U.S. Department of Labor, May 1996: http://www.rufwork.com/110/mats/oshaVisualAids.html
4. Rosenblum, L. D. (2010). *See What I'm Saying: The Extraordinary Powers of Our Five Senses.* New York: W.W. Norton & Company.
5. Stephens, G. J., Silbert, L. J., Hasson, U. (2010). Speaker–Listener Neural Coupling Underlies Successful Communication. *Proceedings of the National Academy of Sciences*, Aug. 2010, 107 (32) 14425–14430; DOI: 10.1073/pnas.1008662107.
6. Ibid.
7. https://www.rochester.edu/pr/Review/V74N4/0402_brainscience.html
8. https://citeseerx.ist.psu.edu/viewdoc/download?doi=10.1.1.720.6969&rep=rep1&type=pdf
9. Dewan, P. (2015). Words Versus Pictures: Leveraging the Research on Visual Communication. *Partnership: The Canadian Journal of Library and Information Practice and Research*, *10*(1). https://doi.org/10.21083/partnership.v10i1.3137

10. MIT: https://news.mit.edu/2014/in-the-blink-of-an-eye-0116
11. https://www.researchgate.net/publication/332380784_How_many_words_do_we_read_per_minute_A_review_and_meta-analysis_of_reading_rate
12. http://misrc.umn.edu/workingpapers/fullpapers/1986/8611.pdf

Chapter 6

1. Harvard Business Review. (2020). How to Get People to Actually Participate in Virtual Meetings.
2. State of the Conversation Report, The Next Best Thing to Being There, Sept. 24, 2018.
3. Ibid.

Chapter 7

1. Harvard Business Review: Getting Virtual Teams Right, (2014), and The Art of Building Trust on Virtual Platforms (2020).
2. The Balance Careers, July 2019: https://www.thebalancecareers.com/what-is-active-listening-2917365

Chapter 8

1. Bain & Company (2020). Virtual B2B Selling Is Here to Stay, June 2020.
2. McKinsey (2020). B2B Decision-Maker Pulse Survey, 8 April 2020 (Article: The B2B digital inflection point: How sales have changed during Covid-19).

About the Authors

About Implement

How can organisations become truly fit for humans and fit for the future? More competitive, adaptable, and sustainable—and more innovative, engaging, and entrepreneurial?

We believe it calls for an uncompromising combination of deep functional and transformational expertise. It also calls for a certain mindset: that all change starts with people and that consulting is, in essence, helping. And it demands we work in small, agile teams committed to creating impact together with our clients.

Headquartered in Copenhagen with offices in Aarhus, Stockholm, Malmo, Oslo, Zurich, and Munich, we are fortunate to count more than 900 colleagues working globally with clients on projects of all shapes, sizes, and ambitions.

Christian Milner Nymand

Christian Milner Nymand is a senior partner at Implement Consulting Group and head of the Commercial Excellence business practice. He specialises in expanding the commercial capabilities and accelerating top line growth of international B2B companies, and leading global sales transformations.

Mante Kvedare
Mante Kvedare is a partner at Implement Consulting Group and a trusted advisor to leading global companies. She specialises in commercial strategy and has extensive experience in supporting international B2C and B2B organisations to design and implement their commercial change initiatives.

Acknowledgements

We would like to thank our global customers for their trust in us to support their virtual transformation journeys. We would also like to thank Ole Kristoffer Bjelland, Lea Charlotte Hellmann, Anna Duus, Michael Ærø, Trine Høstmark Solhaug, and our whole global commercial excellence family at Implement Consulting Group for their support in the creation of this book and for continuously developing our virtual sales concept.

Index